Your Power Pivot

Shifting the Paradigm of Work/Life Empowerment

LS Publishing

ISBN-13: 978-1986352925

ISBN-10: 1986352927

DEDICATION

This work is dedicated to my beautiful and empowered daughters, Lena and Bella, and to my amazing son, Raff. Pivot and see how amazing the world truly is.

Table of Contents:

Chapter 1: Tossing the Junk in Your Trunk (p.13)

Stopping the Struggle

Junk in Your Trunk

Lessons Learned or Repeated

Chapter 2:There is More to Life than Gender Differences(p. 39)

Embracing the Gender Difference and Learning from It

Closing the Salary Gap

Redefining the Glass Ceiling

Chapter 3: Comfortable in Your Own Shoes (p.71)

Defining Authenticity

Being the CEO of Your Life

Lead YOUR Ship; Women's Leadership

Chapter 4:Identifying Your Needs ... Then Versus Now (p.113)

Needs Are for Survival—Wants Make Life Interesting

The Bedroom—Sanctuary or Laundry Room

Wearing Heels in the Boardroom

Chapter 5: Balance the Misnomer: Work/Life Strategies (p.149)

Communication—The Emotional Sabotage

Resilience—The Tigger Effect

More Pie = Energy

Chapter 6: Success is Not a Solo Task (p.187)

Success is a Game of RISK

Build Your Success Team

The Sandbox—Where to Find Other Great Women

Chapter 7: She's Not Just a Pretty Face—Creating the Female Bridge (p.227)

Why Can't We All Just Get Along?

The Gift of Motherhood

Raising the Next Generation of Leaders

Chapter 8: Getting Fired with Style—Exit Strategies (p.253)

You're Fired with Style

Getting Back in the Saddle

Chapter 9: Now Is Your Time, What Will You Do With It? (p.277)

Keeping Your Personal Power

Either Get on My Train or Get Off

References (p.289)

Pivotal Books I Love (p.292)

About the Author

ACKNOWLEDGMENTS

This work would not be possible without the unwavering support and insight of the following people:

Kathleen Burns Kingsbury, you are always in my corner

My Sandbox Team: Maria Lynch and Gina Abudi

The amazing Pivotal Women who shared their power with all my readers

My husband Rico and my three amazing children, for being there and helping me find my cake and sharing it with me.

Pivot:

Noun: a person or thing that is central or important to someone or something else

Verb: to turn on or around a pivotal point

Power Pivot:

Verb: the unique ability to shift perspective—changing the paradigm of work/life empowerment

Power Pivot

Why did I write this work? I have purchased many self-help books only to leave them on the book shelf collecting dust. Sound familiar? One reason they collect dust is their vantage point in business was not mine, thus they did not speak to me or keep my attention, as the scope of the work was too narrow or biased. Simply put, there was a need for a piece of literature that showed women how to take accountability, shift perspective, and apply their own personal power both at work and at home.

I am a case in point, the extraordinary average woman. I am a mom of three, a CEO of a leadership diversity consulting firm, an author, speaker, youth soccer and girls lacrosse coach, adjunct faculty member of the University of New Hampshire System and a great friend and mentor to a few. I love to laugh and cry, have girls' night wine and be present in all that I do. More importantly, I live life to the fullest and have learned how to be empowered both at work and at home, creating harmony.

How, you may ask? By pivoting my perspectives. By seeing things in paradigms and making connections. Nothing in life is truly black or white—they are shades of vantage points.
So a bit more about your author…I graduated from the University of Massachusetts back in 1993, years after joining the United

States Army to pay for college. While attending undergrad, I worked full time to pay my tuition and living expenses. I come from a low- to middle-class dysfunctional family with six siblings (I am the second oldest). Once I graduated college, I started in the field of pharmaceutical sales and, well, the rest is history.

In my professional life I have thrived, even though I have been fired. I have climbed the corporate ladder and also slid off it. Promoted, discriminated against, and looked over.

In my personal life I have suffered the personal loss of my father at a young age, weathered a history of mental and sexual abuse, and battled an eating disorder—yet now I am happily married and have three wonderful children. I coach youth sports both girls and boys, am active in my children's education and have a passion for wine and life. The key to my happiness…**I determined my path and I will show you how to find yours.**

This work is a look at how some women survive and others thrive. It is meant to be a tool in your path to work/life harmony and empowerment. It is meant to be read cover to cover; however, read what you need first.

We start off by examining what helped shape the authentic you, those "aha" pivotal moments that you allowed to define you. Along the way you will learn tips and techniques that will help you shift over some of life's speed bumps. You may find there is some deep self-reflecting work needed and feel a bit nervous or uncomfortable about what you may have learned about yourself—and for that I say… YES! Remember and post this: *In un-comfort comes growth and in growth comes empowerment.* You are also not alone.

Another goal of this work is to say it, to empower you, the reader, to stop hiding what issues or topics make you uncomfortable. Take the taboo-ness of certain areas of our lives off the table. In sections of the work we will be focused on the bedroom and home life strategies, then to relationship communication. We will talk about how we as women need to stop being mean to each other and start helping each other along. My hope is in putting it out there in black and white, maybe, just maybe we as women will stop and empower another along our journey—or at least encourage them to seek help on their own.

Throughout this book there are powerful quotes and comments from other amazing *Pivotal Women* who, like you, seek to thrive or are already in their own thrive mode. These women focus on the needs of all women and then put themselves out there, take risks, identify areas of growth and lead the way. Some of these amazing women you may know, while others are the gems we aspire to be. I hope after briefly meeting these women here, you will follow them and continue on your path. Follow this with *Shifting Paradigms* in each chapter, where you get to dig in deep and explore your own growth and empowerment. Each section has an area for you to explore…you. In the end, the book becomes focused on your own personal growth.

We as women are more than *Just a Pretty Face*…we are unique and powerful creatures of the world, and being that, we need to embrace ourselves and others. We need to teach the next generation, as well as the generation above us, how to change and become empowered. Yes, you guessed where this is going—we need to celebrate with each other how wonderful we are, how empowered we are, and how we get through our challenges together versus alone.

Empowerment is a journey not for the faint of heart, as it takes work, self-awareness, insight, close friends, an openness to see opportunities and a few glasses of wine.
The rewards, however, are boundless.

Cheers,

Lauran Star

www.LauranStar.com

Chapter 1
Tossing the Junk in Your Trunk

When we purge what weighs us down, we find there is room for growth and empowerment.

Lauran Star

Stopping the Struggle

*The best gift we can give ourselves is to stop,
take a deep breath and be open for what is to come next.
For what comes next is your opportunity to thrive.*

Today, life seems about being something or someone we are not. We dress a certain way, behave as we are told, wish to be seen or perceived by others by our outer mask and then wonder why we are misunderstood. We have all heard—*be the best you can be, be authentic, be transformational, be transparent, be defined*—yet all too often what is holding us back from enjoy life is that belief that who we are and what we stand for is not enough.

We find ourselves not being in the moment or present as we are focused on *what we should be versus who we truly are*. There appears to be, as a sub-section of society, a tendency for individuals to be caught in their own "junk" from the past, and they are allowing that garbage to define who they are rather than trusting their own choices to shape themselves. I refer to this as *Junk in Your Trunk*, the stuff that holds you back and throws up barricades. In order for you to become empowered, you need to understand what moments in life shaped you. You cannot be authentic to yourself if you do not understand what made you...you. Personal accountably for the hand you've been dealt will also fall short, as you do not know how to play the game.

Have you ever looked around at your friends or colleagues, the ones that are strong and resilient and wondered, "Wow, nothing seems to drag her/him down. Why are they different from the others who appear to enjoy being a victim?" I have to ask, which one are you? Sure there is a time to wallow, but do you pull your big-girl panties up, or do you survive on being miserable? Do you have friends or colleagues who just love to whine?

> *Strength shows not only the ability to persist,*
> *but also in the ability to start again.*
> *Overcoming traumatic events is hard,*
> *but we always manage to summon the strength to help us move*
> *on and start again.*
> **Ritu Ghatourey**

THRIVING IS A CHOICE

We all have had hardships, some more unique or difficult than others; however, how we deal with those situations shapes how we see the world around us. There is a fluid process in which we transition in life, yet unfortunately it can go both forward and backwards, thus limiting growth. In my mind it looks like this: *we move from hardship to victim...then if we are strong enough we become a survivor...and then we decide. Do we allow the Junk in our Trunk to define us or shape us?*

If it defines us we remain in survivor mode. However, there are quite a few of us that move into thriving mode—as we do not allow the past to define us, as we move forward, it is what helps shape us. Sometimes the best way to stop the struggle is to address it. Write it down and solve the issue—put it to bed.

Shifting Paradigms

If you are one who loves drama or cannot seem to get out of your own way...I have to ask, why? What do you gain? Be honest with yourself here, as the only person who can change you is...you.

What about friendships that bring you down? Do you keep them or toss them? I have a dear friend who gave me the best advice back when I was pregnant with my twins. "If the friendship takes more energy than it is worth, end it. The world is toxic enough." This has furthered into my message, *if caller ID is a better friend then the one on the other end it is time to place some space there.*

There's a beauty about a woman whose confidence comes from experiences. Who knows she can fall, pick herself up, and go on.
Anonymous

EMOTIONAL HIJACKING_____

I note emotions throughout the book, but let us take a look now at what emotions are and can do. In a nutshell, many argue we need emotions to live, I argue we need emotions to connect with others on a deeper level. They make us more dynamic and all encompassing. Emotions are happiness, joy, sadness, anger—well, you get the point. There is a full spectrum of emotions we have and share. One facet of our emotions is self-preservation. Emotions work to keep us safe. One way they do this is...FEAR.

Fear is an emotion, and what an emotion it is. We need to recognize when fear is in play, resulting in what I call emotional sabotage. When fear enters our emotional brain (the amygdala) everything else just shuts down. We struggle to focus on the issues, stand up for ourselves, and keep calm and rational. Fear tells our brain to RUN; however, to come to any kind of resolution, you have to stay.

What does fear look like? In a confrontation or adverse situation, it comes to us on a physical level such as sweaty palms, panting, dizziness or nausea, muscle constriction in case you need to run, dry mouth and, of course, one of my favorite tells, pupil dilation (this is how some poker player know your bluffing).

As for your mind, fear helps drive *phronemophobia*, the fear of thinking. You are no longer listening to anyone around you as your mind quickly tries to get you out of there. Words such as *like*, *ummmm*, and *right* start playing havoc with your communication as your brain needs time to complete its thoughts. The past comes right back in to haunt you. Comments like, "Yes well, remember when you did not complete your expense report seven years ago..."

The key to stopping this emotional sabotage is to address it immediately. Keep in mind, we need to respect fear as it does have its role—imagine being fearless in a gunfight, and you have no gun.

So how do we neutralize fear in situations where it adds no value?

SHIFTING PARADIGMS

Take a moment and breathe. Remember, fear changes the body dynamic, and usually the first to go is oxygen. Breathing works two-fold: it replenishes Oxygen and gives you a few moments to think and calm down.

Center yourself. I center myself by touching my middle finger and thumb together. When I am in conflict and can plan ahead, I have a soft stone that is shaped like a heart, which I hold or keep in a pocket. Crazy as this sounds, it centers me. Others may call this *mindfulness*:—where you focus on being present through your core. I am a huge fan of Ellen Langer on this topic; she offers a wide range of books including the bestseller, *Mindfulness*.

Remind yourself that you are not confronting a lion...only a kitten. Pivoting your perspective helps you and your mind cope. Awareness that this is a fear paradigm will give you strength. Go ahead and talk to yourself about why fear cannot play right now.

If fear really has a strong hold on you seek out a professional, or read a few books on emotional stress relief techniques. One such technique is Tapping. These Emotional Freedom Techniques appear to work nicely as the tapping interrupts the fear impulses on the brain. One such work is *The Tapping Solution: A Revolutionary System for Stress-Free Living* by Nick Ortner.

Focus on just the facts, and write them down. Activate your Reticular Activating System (RAS) as it will bring you a bit more focus. The Reticular Activating System (RAS) is the brain's filtering system where the brain shakes out what to or what not to focus on. When we allow the RAS to become activated either through acknowledgement and writing information down you allow the RAS to focus elsewhere. If you do not address the RAS focal points they just cycle and spin until you do. Have you ever woken up in the middle of the night and found your mind to be very noisy? This is the RAS trying to grab your attention. Keep a notepad by your bed and write down whatever is keeping you awake. Purge your RAS and you will be able to fall back asleep.

If you can step away and return to the issue later, identify the worst case scenarios or poor outcomes. What is this thing we fear? Then identify the winning outcomes (hint: write the winning ones down).

We gain strength, and courage, and confidence by each experience in which we really stop to look fear in the face...we must do that which we think we cannot.
Eleanor Roosevelt

With fear we have a choice, we can either let it play along or we can shut it down. Don't let fear win. If you are trying to stop your struggles, I bet fear has a hand in the mess.

The Junk in Your Trunk

The saying 'one man's junk is another man's treasure' is incorrect...
Junk is junk and should be tossed out and never picked through again.

Junk in your trunk is the mindset that if you hold on to garbage of your past, it will have a negative effect on your ability to be in the moment. It is more than those little life struggles repeating themselves as the junk can literally dump all over you and others in your life. It rears its head by scapegoating, as some people let it define them, and they wear it as a badge of honor resulting in excuses. I know that may seem a bit harsh, but stay with me.

The *junk in your trunk* is a series of life episodes that happened to you when you were a kid, or when you were in college, or even now when you're an adult, that can quickly become the anchor that holds you back from achieving success, happiness, empowerment, or any other desire you have. The *junk* helps define you as a victim as you move into survivor.

Examples:

"I got fired from my last job, so I am not good at leadership."

"I have a mental illness, so I am not employable."

"I am getting a divorce, thus I am a bad person and everyone is now talking about me."

"I was abused as a child, therefore I am unworthy of love."

"My parents divorced when I was a kid, so I have a hard time with commitment."

We all know talking about your past junk is therapeutic; however, if your junk is getting in the way of your happiness, do something about it. Yes, it may even require professional help. Keep in mind that in seeking help, you are empowering yourself to move forward, close a circle, and heal. Seeking help is not a weakness. It takes strength to understand you cannot do or solve the junk by yourself. Mostly, it takes courage and strength to deal with the past.

You know that cliché saying: *No one can make you happy but you*? Voila. It is so true and we all have emotional scars. I believe we call that life. Look, everybody has junk in their trunk, but some allow that junk to shape them, and others allow it to define who they are.

Life shrinks or expands in proportion to one's courage.
Anais Nin

My Junk and What I Learned

I came from a typical dysfunctional, nomadic, low-income family with divorced parents. I even lived in a tent for several months as a child—it was a wild adventure. Canned spaghetti was an all-time favorite food because it beat starving. Children have little to no idea if their family is dysfunctional, but they know when they're low income. For some, this is the junk that shapes them. It foreshadows their work, as they may find the passion and fight to change homelessness or food pantry programs, creating solutions from their past—BRAVO.

However, for me that was not challenging enough. When I was in the fifth grade, I had the most sacred trust violated by a person sworn to protect me. My stepfather sexually abused me until I was in eighth grade. It was a secret based on my need to keep my family together. As a child, I feared if I told, he would leave and so would the house, the food, and any love I could scrap for—it would all be my fault. So I kept quiet, kept the action and memories all to myself, and became a "compliant good girl." I always did as I was told; some would even say I became my mother's favorite. I learned to place the needs of my family above all else, even when the maturity kicked in and I realized the action itself was wrong. That blame was not for me to hold onto. Adding fuel to the anger, years later I learned she, my own mother, was aware of the abuse yet decided to choose the bottle over me.

Looking back now as an adult, I am so very proud of that little girl I was. You see, back then I could have chosen to let the years of abuse destroy me, could have ended my life, chosen drugs, and simply just given up. Instead, maybe because of the dysfunction, I decided to shift my own perspective. You have to understand, when this all came to a boil, my mom threw me out of her bedroom, called me horrid names, and claimed to disown me. It was at that moment, crying in my room, that I decided I was in charge of my own life. I was going to graduate high school and then college and get as far away from this environment as I could. I would be whoever I needed to be to survive that environment until I could get away.

Now let's be real—I am by no way saying it was all a bed of roses, because trust me, I was fighting for my life. There were times when the trauma defined me, my relationships, and my actions. While in college and on my own, I sought to create a solid support system of friends and continued to grow. I was then a victim and then, through therapy, a survivor. True to survivor form, I wore my survivorship like a badge. It defined me, my relationships, and even my work. I joined the United States Armed Forces as a means to teach myself self-defense. It also helped me pay for college. I received my Bachelor's degree in Psychology and applied what I had learned, and then I went into therapy. This is where the real work began. Looking back now, I see how at times I still hid my head in the sand to protect others first. I was not ready to move into thriving mode.

My corporate work was playing in a man's sandbox as I worked in sales leadership for several Fortune 500 pharmaceutical/medical and biotech organizations. I became stronger and created a hard shell. I played like a man and shoved the real me down. Deep inside I was protecting the little girl, yet all others saw was this fierce businesswoman. I let my softer side get tucked away in a box as I became the achiever. In my personal life I married a man who loved that strong independent side of me as that strength is part of who I am.

Was I happy? A little. Fulfilled? A little less. A whole person living her dreams? Not even close. Then, amazingly I became pregnant and gave birth to my beautiful son followed by the incredible birth of my twin girls 18 months later. Shortly after the birth of my daughters, while holding them and playing with my son, I came to revelation: as blessed as I was, I was living as a survivor. I was letting my junk define who I was. Giving birth reminded me that my junk not only affected me it also affected my children and husband in advertency.

It was that moment when I decided to move from surviving to thriving, to truly toss the junk in my trunk. I burned the journals I had written, ended relationships with toxic family members, tossed old photos that reminded me of the abuse, spoke with family that may have known or should know and see truly who was in my corner, who had my back and who did not. I realized it would have been easier to stay in survivor mode as the abuse, in my case, could be utilized as a scapegoat. However, honestly you have to ask yourself, where does that all get me? A pity party for one, or a pity party for those around you that you drag into it. Instead of sitting back and wallowing or surviving, I chose to push forward—to become empowered and to thrive.

We all have the ability to be empowered and happy, to move forward. All it takes is a matter of taking a deep breath, looking around and shifting your perspective, analyzing what happened and then understanding how it makes you stronger. You have to want to dig in deeper and lean towards forgiveness of both yourself and others. This is hard work and not done overnight. **New journals** need to be started; conversations and self-awareness need to develop. Your past and present actions beg to be given attention as you begin to understand the whys. A wonderful benefit of tossing your junk: your personal self-awareness rises. You begin to see how your actions and the actions of others effect just about everything. This is hard work; however, the end results are so worth it.

There is clarity and peace as you discover how not to allow the little things in life get in the way.

Remember, your junk is yours; therefore other people's junk is theirs. **Don't judge or take on other people's junk.** Recognize that others who have junk that is holding them down will see your strength. It is not uncommon for them to attempt to pull you into their junk. It is your fortitude they are looking for, but it is still theirs to deal with.

How we each react or respond to our own junk is personal. Some women attack their junk and move quickly through it while others may try to divert, go around, or avoid it unless their junk is called to attention. There is no right or wrong way in tossing your garbage.

SO HOW DO WE TOSS THE JUNK

First, know when to ask for help with your junk. Ladies, you are not alone—we all have junk in our trunk that needs to be tossed. Some of my closest friends came to light when I expressed a need of help, when I was vulnerable and support was warranted. You need external support when the junk hinders you from happiness, when it defines you. You need to move from victim to survivor. Sometimes you can do this all by yourself; other times you may need professional help, like a therapist. A therapist can help you understand the issues you're facing and the impact it has had on your life. Keep in mind the junk is yours to deal with or not in the way you deal with it.

Once you face your junk, you then move from victim to survivor. A survivor takes time and work. You can expect to journal, shift thoughts to the "what ifs," and begin to heal from your junk. You may even begin to feel emotions or thoughts you had bottled up. Conversations may become difficult and then freeing. Write it all down as you are now on your journey of growth. It certainly helps having another to keep it all in perspective.

Going from survivor to one who is thriving tends to be a bit easier as the healing aspect is almost done. You now re-approach the past with a different set of glasses on. I like to call these my "purple glasses," as the color change signifies new beginnings. Your perspective shifts as you understand what you learned from the junk and then apply it. It is asking those questions—what did I learn from this, who benefited, what decisions in life have been shaped by this junk, am I happy with these decisions, and if not what will I do about it today—that will facilitate our perspective shift. In this transition, a personal coach can help you move forward by helping you uncover what you already knew.

But I like being a survivor…. That is fine—if you are happy there, stay there. It is your choice. Just be aware that if you are in survivor mode, it may hold you back from thriving as you may wear the survivor button as a badge of honor. In survivor mode, everything you do has a taint of the past attached, like the nagging question left unsaid. In survivor mode, your personal growth can only go so far.

The benefit of thriving simply put is a happier life. When you are thriving, the past is just that—the past. It cannot hold you down. When you are thriving, you see you are in charge and are not manipulated as easily as when you were in survivor mode. You see the beauty in life without the taint of garbage. Your health may improve.

SHIFTING PARADIGMS

Have you ever sat down and looked over your past and asked the question:

- What is holding you back?
- Where do you seem to struggle again and again?
- Do you address these struggles or just let them sit there?
- What keeps you awake at night?
- Do I have junk that defines me?
- How did my junk shape me rather than define me?
- What decisions have I made that were junk based?
- What would life be like if the junk were gone?
- Do I like my junk?

- Who can help me toss this junk once and for all?

Self-awareness of your past junk is critical in the growth process of tossing that junk. It can help us understand why we react the way we do in every situation. It also encompasses the skill of regulating the subsequent reactions of a situation to achieve the best results.

Lessons Learned or Repeated

At the end of the day, our greatest enemy can be our unwillingness to be open and honest with ourselves.

Have you ever found yourself in the same situation, different day? This is in large part because the junk in your trunk is still there, meaning you have yet to learn the lesson that the junk provided. Yes, the junk in your trunk can provide a valuable life lesson IF you decide to move from surviving into thriving. However, once you decide to toss the junk, you need to move forward and stop repeating lessons already learned. While in survivor mode, we are still focused on the event or trauma. We still identify with the past issues at hand. Once in thrive mode you can see past the issues, think more clearly and begin to assimilate lessons around the junk. Example: my junk, as described above. In post-survivor mode, I learned how to become more resilient as I did not allow the abuse to hold me back. I also learned how to be proud of myself when adversity faced me as I did not cower or run. I learned conflict management skills in dealing with emotional family members (conflict is useless if emotions are the driver—take emotions out. More on that in Chapter 5).

The biggest lesson I learned: I found my voice. I found the real Lauran Star. Once I addressed the junk (after the birth of my children) and tossed it out of my life, I learned that being a survivor was not enough, as today I am thriving. I also pass those messages on to my children and all who are close to me.

Always embrace life lessons, because nothing ever goes until it has taught us what we need to know in life, if we run a hundred miles an hour to the other end of the continent in order to get away from the obstacle; we find the very same problem waiting for us when we arrive.
Kemmy Nola

Here is what we know about repeating the past: until we truly understand the situation or issue, as well as the *how* and *why* we react the way we do, we just repeat until we get it right. This skill set is known as *personal clarity,* or self-awareness, and it is learnable. Once personal clarity around an issue is apparent, we move into *discovery* and then *growth* (this is the tossing part).

PUTTING IT ON THE TABLE_____

While the process of moving from clarity to growth sounds simple, we all know it is not.

Personal Clarity: The critical component in halting the repetition of life lessons is identifying what they were/are.

- What are those moments around us that should make us stop and think? That give you pause? Do you note them or just walk away? Become aware of those instances, how you reacted and what you said, then examine later to see if there are any lessons there.

- What past situations are you still holding on to? "My parents divorced when I was a child so I suck at relationships." As the song says, let it go. Why hold on to stuff that is better off tossed out? Write these situations down and then throw them away.

- Do you hold grudges or let them go? "I have this one friend with whom I always feel like I am in competition, even though there is not competition. Maybe it is all in my head." You have a choice: confront or walk way. Regardless, at least you will have closure.

- What lesson or issues keep coming to the forefront of your life? "Why do people always give me a hard time about my timing? It's not like I am always late. Give me a break." Maybe there is a problem that you need to address. Stop sticking your head in the sand and making excuses.

- When problems arise, is there a theme? "I always seem to fight around money with my partner. He thinks..." Theme issues are problems that you tend to run from. Confront and put them to bed.

- Who defines you? Are you authentic to yourself or are you living your life by others' rules and dreams?

The key to personal clarity...**you MUST be honest with yourself** first and you must want to do the work. Some reach personal clarity by being forced into it—being pushed beyond all return or backed into a wall—then deciding to deal with the issues and moving forward. On the flip side, for some, pushing can result in more junk in your trunk; again, the decision is yours to make. Others have learned to see issues before they become problems and then address their own personal clarity accordingly. Once you have gone through this process, in the end you'll understand the issue and why you react the way you do.

This is not an overnight step when first reaching for personal clarity; however, like a muscle the more you flex it the faster it builds. It is more than moving on from an issue, however, as it is looking at an issue through clear glasses, seeing both sides as well as alternative approaches for growth.

Discovery: So now that you have personal clarity, what did you learn? The discovery aspect can be both enlightening as well as truth seeking. This is the phase where we understand *why* we responded the way we did. We need to dig in deeper and hold a mirror up to see the true reflection. If you struggle with discovery, find a good personal coach who will be your sounding board.

Ask yourself the following questions:

- Why did you repeat the event?
- What was your initial action?
- What would you like that action to have been/what would you do differently?
- How is this similar to other issues in your life?
- Who are the players? Sometimes we repeat lessons because of the players, not the issue.
- Who has the power, you, the situation, or someone else?

In discovery, open yourself to seeing the power dynamic at play: who has it and why. Often we repeat a lesson out of power struggles. We fight the same battle a different day looking for a different power shift. The kicker: only YOU can give away your power. If another takes power from you, you allowed it. Hold on to your power by noting you are not giving it away.

SHIFTING PARADIGMS

What helped shape you? I encourage you to ask yourself that question. What shaped you, and do you want a pity party around it? Or are you able to take those tools and put them to work for you?

The final aspect of not repeating lessons is growth. What did you learn from the last lesson and did you apply it? One

may need to rephrase the lesson to learn the meaning.
Example: if you are constantly fighting about money with your partner, is it really about your spending or is it deeply based on how you view money? Once you discover the true issue, growth occurs when you then do something about it. When you recognize the issue for what it is, address it and then—you guessed it—learn and move on.

One of the fastest ways to stop the cycle of repeating lessons is to journal—write it down and then address it.

This does not have to take hours to do; sometimes just a quick note will do the trick. Journaling/writing down information activates the Reticular Activating System (RAS) in the brain. (This is the brain's filtering system where the brain shakes out what to or what not to focus on.) When we write something down, the RAS notes that this information is important and needs to be acted on, thus reducing repeating lessons already learned. Journaling truly is a gift you can give yourself and a wonderful tool in discovery and growth.

Chapter 2

There is More to Life than Gender Differences

If we decide to allow gender to determine our path, we may find those stereotypes becoming self-fulfilling prophecies

Embracing the Gender Difference and Learning from It

When we decide to allow gender to determine our fate, we are blind to our own weakness.

Today's business world demands we all work together. Regardless of cultural backgrounds, language barriers, and gender differences, the top companies that thrive have learned to blend their team—creating diversity and inclusion not just in the workplace but also in the marketplace. It is not an "us versus them" business world anymore. Honestly, I am not sure it ever was, yet as women progressed in this world, some decided burning the bra received more attention than digging in deep, learning from each other, and getting the job done.

I am a feminist. Now let me define that for you as some of you may be sitting back and either cringing at that statement or cheering. According to the Merriam-Webster Dictionary:

Fem·i·nism, noun: the belief that men and women should have equal rights and opportunities; the theory of the political, economic, and social equality of the sexes; organized activity on behalf of women's rights and interests.

I define this term for you in part because as women, are we not all feminists, all a part of a sisterhood that wants the best for each other? Do we not believe we should all have equal rights? We are, after all, in the United States of America where equality is at the forefront of democracy. Are not our sons, brothers, and husbands feminists? Do they not wish for your happiness at work and home? Sure, some may show it in a more public way, but in the end the vast majority desires this equality. When was the last time your husband or brother said, "You should work harder than I do ...you are a woman"? It comes down to pivoting how you see feminism and gender differences.

Men and women are different both at home and at work. We both have very different strengths and skill sets that allow us to be authentic to who we are. We lead, communicate, think, problem solve, and process information individually. Nonetheless, we can all learn from each other, rather than fight with each other. If we embrace these variations we learn new morsels of knowledge and traits.

I come from a male-dominated business world. It is where I learned my business acumen and then created my own authentic leadership style combining both genders. It is one of the reasons I can communicate, manage conflict, and negotiate to the level that I do. I do not see gender in the light others do. I instead look for the strengths each person brings to the table. I call this there personal value statement. It is what makes them who they are and the talent they have accumulated thus far.

The day will come when man will recognize woman as his peer, not only at the fireside, but in councils of the nation. Then, and not until then, will there be the perfect comradeship, the ideal union between the sexes that shall result in the highest development of the race.
Susan B. Anthony

I DO NOT SEE GENDER_____

There was a time where color in the workplace was supposed to be blind. We hired without seeing "color" or ethnic diversity. The theory behind being colorblind was to learn from each individual as to their strengths, divergence, and character. We were not to see and then judge by color. Those little biases we learned as we were growing up were to be placed on a shelf for the outside world. The same holds true for gender. If we stop looking at what the gender is and start exploring the level of distinction, similarities and variations, we can then learn and adapt to them. This is inclusion.

We need to move from diversity in the workplace to inclusion. Gender inclusion will result in the strengths of each individual person being brought into the workplace. Let me shake this a bit more.

In searching for the definitions of diversity and inclusion I must acknowledge the Royal Bank of Canada (http://www.rbc.com/diversity/what-is-diversity.html) and their work in this area. They define diversity and inclusion as follows; "Diversity in broad terms, is any dimension that can be used to differentiate groups and people from one another. It means respect for and appreciation of differences in ethnicity, gender, age, national origin, disability, sexual orientation, education, and religion.

Inclusion however *is a state of being valued, respected and supported. It's about focusing on the needs of every individual and ensuring the right conditions are in place for each person to achieve his or her full potential. Inclusion should be reflected in an organization's culture, practices and relationships that are in place to support a diverse workforce.*

While organizations are focused on diversity, especially on the leadership boards for gender equality, it is inclusion where all will thrive. It is not enough to just have the numbers in place. Fifty percent diversity means nothing if inclusion is missing.

Genders have different strengths and assets. We need to explore and create a positive environment for each person to grow.

HOW WE ARE DIFFERENT

Leadership style—today in business, there is a need and desire for more transformational leadership. Organizations are screening for finesse in this arena as the business world itself is now outside the box. However there are plenty of opportunities for transactional leadership within an organization.

Transformational leadership is the ability to lead by inspiring. To inspire and motivate others toward greatness. This leader is trustworthy and ethical, is a role model to all, and empowers others to take ownership of their work. They are not without fault, but they are flexible enough to overcome shortcomings and to embrace accountability. They are big-picture leaders and feel there is no box.

According to Bass (2008), the counter style is *transactional leadership*. This style focuses on the role of supervision, organization, and group performance. Its leaders reward follow-through based on both rewards and punishments. Leaders using the transactional approach are not looking to change the future, they are looking to merely keep things the same.

That all being said, which style is feminine and which is masculine? Is there a gender for each style? According to Project Globe, an international, long-term, multi-method, multi-phase research program focused on international leadership and organizational practices, it was found in the Western culture men were more transactional leaders and women tended to be transformational leaders from an organizational leadership style (House et al., 2001). There is more data that support these findings. Women tend to be more transformational in leadership style and men transactional.

Does that make women better leaders? Nope. It comes down to what you do with that style and the impact it has on others. If you are now starting to think outside the gender box, you may realize that leadership styles can be learned and adjusted depending on the situation. Gender really has no input unless you let it.

How else are we different, and how can we build on that difference_____

Men and women have a smorgasbord of divergences, from how hormones affect the brain to how they attack business and home life issues. We are a variation, and no matter how much we want to play like men, we cannot, so stop trying. Instead, look at the deviations and build upon their strengths.

I love Shaunti Feldhahn's work in *For Women Only* and *For Men Only*. I have read both books and love how she adapts skills and the best techniques both genders have to offer. If you read one, you have to read the other.

Communication: Women tend to communicate from the heart. We tell tons of stories with plenty of details. Men, on the other hand, tend to focus on the facts first, details last. Even in written communication there is a vast difference. Men typically read only the first few lines, whereas women want more story.

Problem solving: Men approach problem solving as a way to show off their skills and competency's. *Problems are opportunities in disguise,* so says my husband. They attack a problem from a paper aspect, write down the pros and cons as well as what they know as fact. Women, on the other hand, approach from an emotional standpoint. We tend to see the bigger picture, the implications outside the issue. Now imagine a think tank with both genders...and welcome to the Central Intelligence Agency. They utilize both brains in problem solving.

Thinking: Women tend to be more intuitive thinkers, where the box can disappear. Men are a bit more linear. In the forms of multitasking, women win hands down. Studies have demonstrated the female brain has a capacity to process more firing arms. I believe women are stronger at multitasking because we have to be, especially moms. Let us face it—we just get more practice at it. Men, however, focus from task to task or from problem to problem.

Empathy: Women have this hands down. Sometimes to the extreme. I work on my empathy in large part because I have this in excess. Example: recently I went for a pedicure, and on the television was the movie *Charlie St. Cloud*. I could not stop crying, not hormonal crying, as I could feel the pain the family suffered, the confusion, and the anger. It took the stylist asking me if I had recently lost someone to somewhat pull me back. Empathy is an area women can get lost in. More often than not we need to work on keeping it in check versus developing it. However, some women could use a bit of work there too (wink).

My point is, we all work together so why not learn from each other? I learned how to negotiate my salary from my male counterparts, as well as how to directly make decisions, and you can too. All you need to do is ask.

Closing the Salary Gap

Salary is indirectly the measurement of how YOU perceive YOUR OWN self-worth, nothing more.

According to the 2014 United States Census Bureau, the gender salary gap is as accordingly: women make $0.77 on the dollar to men's salary. This equates to a decrease in weekly overall pay of $749.00 or yearly at $8,993.00. Now, what I am about to write may make you uncomfortable or dislike me, and yes some will shout out against my next comment and take the opportunity to let me know how unflavored my leadership is. However, the #1 reason for the gap is **women do not ask for more**. Yes, it is our own fault. I am sure I will receive plenty of flak for this comment regardless it is true.

I spent fifteen years in corporate America working with several Fortune Top 100 organizations in leadership roles and not once was the comment, *Hey hire a women because we can pay her less* or *If the candidate is a female give her 15-20% less salary*. What I did hear, however, was an overwhelming lack of negotiation skills from women. Hey, I myself have been known to hire a female for less than her male counterpart. Why, you may wonder? He negotiated, she did not, and I, working at the time in corporate America, had a budget to keep. Directly put, salary negotiation is business, it is not personal.

Today there are now talks of state and federal referenda focused on closing this gap based on the increase of minimum wage. I myself am not sure how this will shift the gap if women do not empower themselves to ask for what they are worth. No program or policy will work and why should it unless we are looking at just placing a bandage on the real issue.

Any given salary is based on worth; it is not a gift nor is it personal. If you look at your salary, ask yourself: Are they getting what they are paying for? If the answer is yes, then you did an all right job negotiating. If the answer is no, then work on negotiating, and if your response is Hell Yes, then you have nailed the skill. This is how businesses gain information on what salary demand is for any given task. Is the company getting what they are paying for—the questions above can be applied here too.

Think for a moment...we are a competitive and capitalistic country forged on gaining the advantage. Organizations already have in place salary markers for job roles/titles. There are ranges set for the majority of positions within companies. If we open the salary view as to who is getting paid what, companies will have to place a price tag on talent and skills that are immeasurable. Those skills include negotiation, communication, empathy, emotional intelligence, personal power, influence, visionary leadership, and more. How do we measure who has more? The notion that two candidates are in fact equal, regardless of gender and/or ethnicity, is ridiculous. You are an individual and therefore bring a unique variety of skills and areas of development that are all yours. You should be paid for these immeasurable skills.

Example*:*

Candidate A and B both have the same degree, work experience, and skills required as defined in the job description. We can only hire one. How do we then decide? Yes, it is based on the skills that are immeasurable. Regardless of gender, let's say candidate A is selected, and this same candidate is strong in negotiation and communication (one of the reasons we hired them). They negotiate the job at a higher salary, and we the organization have the option of keeping or passing. What we don't do is offer the position to both and see who comes in lower or does not negotiate.

If we take gender out of the equation, would we scream "salary discrepancy!"?

If candidate A decides they like the base salary and they do not negotiate, do we yell "gender gap in salary!"?

Seems to me...if it is a woman, we do. Yet truly the issue at hand is not salary gap, it is the skills in communication and negotiation that is the real problem, as well as what we bring to the table and show off.

Furthermore, some organizations are looking at salary standardization, and I say absolutely not. My fear with salary standardization is women will still not learn how to take ownership of their own personal worth, and negotiation. The end result will be the drive for competition in the workforce will decrease. Salary standardization will result in an overall reduction in the skills that drive organizations into success. As an avid learner part of what motivates me to continue to grow is knowledge – the other part is reward. Imagine if my communication skills or depth in leadership work no longer equated in the salary arena. Why would anyone bother to go to such depth? Skill negotiation does not come with a set price tag, it boils down to perception. I expect to get paid my worth as determined by me, not by big business.

SALARY NEGOTIATION

It is about your financial accountability to yourself. It is what you see your business worth to an organization. In all my years in corporate, to my knowledge, I was never underpaid or paid less because I was a woman. In fact, it was just the opposite, as I tended to be the top earner. Why? Self-value and negotiation. I should also note I learned how to negotiate from men.

I entered the workforce in the 1990s during and after serving in the United States Army Reserve. I was surrounded by men and then decided I wanted to go into sales (yet another male-dominated field). So when it came to negotiation skills, being surrounded by successful men, I used that as an asset and asked how they got the salary they wanted. Keep in mind, not all men are good at negotiation; however, I teamed up with those who were.

What I Learned
- Always ask for more, at least 10-15% more than offered.
- Understand the value I bring to the organization.
- Understand the market demand and pay scale.
- Everything is negotiable, from salary to time off, benefits to stock options.

These four tips have stayed with me, and they work.

Regardless of salary or any contract, I get paid what I deem my worth. They come full circle in the process and rely heavily on your own personal confidence and communication skills. What surprised me is how often even top earning executives have left money on the table due to the lack of asking, regardless of gender; however, women do tend to leave more.

Stop being thankful and start being accountable to yourself and what you offer!

Here is how it all comes together_____

Always ask for more: Typically when a job is posted there is a salary range, unless noted in the original posting on salary requirements. This range is anywhere from 10-15% up or down. The lesson then makes sense to ask for 10-15% more than what is offered. However, be sure you are worth the increase, meaning before you ask for more, you have to understand what you bring to the table. Do not limit yourself to just 15% if you are worth more. If the organization sees your value, they will pay for it. Make sure you can identify what that asset is as it will be part of your push back for more tools.

Understand what you bring to the table/organization: While you may have many skills in your toolbox, which ones are the most important for the company's growth? What skills outside the job task can you offer? What can you negotiate with on your resume? This is the "why I will rock above the job listed" aspect of you. To understand this, you need to focus on what those are. What in your resume makes you stand out? Often in an interview, these are subconsciously highlighted for you by the person doing the interview. Statements like "your leadership ability will prove to be a huge asset" or "judging from your success in sales, your selling approach works." These are negotiation pieces when asking for more money or time off and should be included in your thank you letter after an interview.

Understand the market demand and pay scale: When you are interviewing for a position, a wise candidate comes prepared. What is the market (job, sales, economic) landscape look like? Are there hundreds of qualified applicants or just a few? What will the position bare in regards to salary? Do an Internet search asking, "what is the average salary for a Vice President of Sales and Marketing?" The results may surprise you. To date, I have a team of individuals I work with both hourly and salaried. I understand talent has a price—it is how I sell myself, thus it is imperative I understand the market of employment and salary scales. When demand is high and supply is low, the price for talent is high and vice versa. It is the law of supply and demand.

Everything is negotiable, from salary to time off, benefits to stock options: If your salary requirement is rejected, go back and uncover the why behind the no. It may be something they are not seeing or you have not shown yet. If the rejection is due to budgets, then ask for something else. Look at benefits as a salad; do you want more lettuce (money), cucumbers (vacation time) tomatoes (stock options), dressing (educational benefits) etc.? What can the company add on to entice you to take the position?

What if they rescind their offer? Yes this may happen, however if it does then they did not see your worth and trust me you never would have made it up. When I first started coaching women in this area I heard over and over again how they believe if they proved themselves in the workplace they would see a larger raise thus shortening the salary gap. *Hmmmm* NOPE – why would an organization pay you more for what you did not negotiate in the first place? Think of it this way, your starting salary includes everything you bring to the organization on day one – no going back. Thus there is no back pay for a skill that was overlooked.

We need to remember not only is the company interviewing you – you are interviewing the company. If they do not value you today (when they are trying to look shiny) they will not tomorrow when the glamour has worn off.

Women need to move from the place of thankfulness for the job to valuing our own person. We need to take accountability for our own history for lacking the skills for negation and learn how to get what we desire. Simple enough to do...ask those around you who are good at winning transaction, regardless of their gender, how they do it. We need to move past the male versus female salary gap as this is an excuse for women to be underpaid.

The same holds true when asking for a raise, albeit the dynamic is a bit different. In asking for a raise, the proof of what you can and can't do is already decided. You will need to further demonstrate additional skills or willingness to take on more responsibility to earn the increase. According to the Social Security Administration, the average Cost of Living Adjustment (COLA) for 2015 will be 1.7%. Here is a hint: if your company is giving you a 2% salary gain, they only see your value at .3%. I am amazed how many men and women do not look at the COLA numbers and then bring the awareness to the raise discussion. Maybe I am cynical or jaded, however I always took the COLA and added seven percent to it for my meets raise. While I may have landed at five percent from time to time, others were still at three.

SHIFTING PARADIGMS_____

Keep and up to date resume running, listing all the new strengths or tasks you have uncovered during your gainful employment. When it comes time to negotiate your raise create the famous "that a girl" file that you can bring with you to demonstrate why you are worth the seven to ten percent above COLA raise.

Keep Emotions out of the equation:

Emotions have no business in work finances. We as women need to learn and appreciate that statement. Remember this is not personal – it is business. If you can take the emotions out and replace them with your value, you will come out right where you should be.

The salary gap is a self-fulfilling prophesy as it serves as an excuse for women not to learn how to negotiate effectively.

Pivotal Woman

Here is what an amazing colleague and thought leader on Women's Wealth had to say about the compensation gap:

Q: How can women shift the compensation gap in the workplace?

Kathleen Burns Kingsbury's Answer: Understand your money mindset and how this influences your ability to ask for and get paid your worth. It is up to each and every woman to negotiate her salary as part of a collective effort to close the gender pay gap. This is complicated as women receive mixed messages about asking for money and being profit-motivated. The bottom line is you need to leave your emotions at the doorstep when asking for a raise and focus on how you add real value to the organization.

Kathleen Burns Kingsbury, Wealth Psychology Expert and Author of *How to Give Financial Advice to Women, How to Give Financial Advice to Couples & Breaking Money Silence.*

Lauran Star

Re-defining the Glass Ceiling

The glass ceiling is so 1990s.
It is time to stop making excuses and excel where we want to excel.

Let me ask you a question: do you believe there is a glass ceiling where you work?

If we stop and define The Glass Ceiling, according to Wikipedia (n.d. 2014), *a **glass ceiling** is a political term used to describe the unseen, yet unbreakable barrier that keeps minorities and women from rising to the upper rungs of the corporate ladder, regardless of their qualifications or achievements.*

This term also came to light in 1986 when the female generational workforce first started to aspire to leadership and equality. Keep in mind, as women were entering the workforce at an aggressive rate, men already were there, and their skill set base was established. The economy was also driven by transactional leadership, a more male-dominated style. Hence, "bitch" (hate this word, it means a female dog, not a successful leader) came into play as women struggled to be authentic to their own style, so they borrowed a more aggressive transactional approach to leadership and business.

I have to then ask…to my earlier question—if you answered yes, you believe there is a glass ceiling at your employment, (1) what is the evidence of said ceiling beyond the lack of women being promoted? (2) What are you doing about it? And (3) Why are you still there?

PUTTING IT IN PERSPECTIVE: WOMEN IN THE WORKFORCE AND LEADERSHIP

Over 75% of Fortune 500 companies have leadership diversity programs in place. Are they working? What we can see is they are focusing on leadership skills and frameworks from the male perspective. Pepsi Company has done a remarkable job promoting and preparing their female executives for success, and they are not alone. Their success is in the inclusion not diversity within the leadership teams.

Research demonstrates *once women start getting promoted in the workforce, their promotion possibility did not significantly differ from men* (Baxter & Wright, 2000)—a counter argument for the glass ceiling. To date, research is showing *little significant glass ceiling effect in the United States market space for advancement* (Baxter & Wright, 2000, Weinberger, 2011); *however, the excuse of a glass ceiling while determining what exactly it does is strongly present* (Russo, Giovanni, and Hassink, 2012). Advancement is happening, ladies, we just need to open our eyes to see it and stop making excuses for what holds us, individually, back.

In the United States, women hold 52% of professional-level jobs with 14.6% at the executive level officers. However, only *4.6% of Fortune 500 companies have female CEOs* (Warner, 2014). Here is where we need to work harder. Companies are desperate to hire female CEOs—heck, we hold the financial purse strings in the United States; thus, it makes strong business sense. That being the case, however, there appears to be a shortage of talent, meaning women who have reached the level of CEO have done the job and are now looking to move to another company. Women tend to be loyal to their organization especially if they were "gifted" with promotions. I argue where efforts need to be focused is in training both men and women. If we want more female CEO, there needs to be a focus on training and advancement than fosters inclusion and skills.

Here is where we play: looking at industry-specific female diversity, the financial services industry has a female ratio of 54.2%, with 12.4% of that in executive officers, 18.3% on board directors, yet no CEOs (Warner, 2014). In the healthcare and social assistance sandbox, women dominated the labor pool at 78.4% with 14.6% in executive officers, 12.4% on board of directors, and again no CEOs (Warner, 2014).

Women in US corporate boards have been stuck between 12.1 and 12.3% over the past decade with only 17% representation on Fortune 500 boards. This number has not budged in eight years. We seem to be stuck. We need to stop blaming our lack of advancement and start uncovering the skills or talents needed to move forward. To ask a harder question – as advancement is a choice – how do organizations entice women to want advancement? Where is the silver spoon in advancement?

I am not saying there is no glass ceiling, as there are organizations that unconsciously hold women back from advancing. However, I argue organizations that have a "glass ceiling" effectively do so unconsciously. When I was discriminated against for a leadership position within a past Fortune 500 company, my claims brought forth education. They were not aware their General Business Unit was 97% white male. The business structure was dysfunctional and leaking money. Actions taken were illegal. And their largest mistake was thinking I would go away. I do so love to make noise—especially after I informed them what they were doing was a violation of the Civil Rights Act of 1964 Title VII.

Business today has demonstrated women hold the purchasing power in households; thus, it would make sense to have women in leadership roles providing direction to an organization as to how women will purchase. According to the US Department of Education, women make up 57% of all students earning bachelor's degrees and 60% of students earning master's degrees. Their better education has led to better jobs and better pay. Today, 48% of working wives/mothers provide at least half of their household income, with 30% of working wives/mothers earning more than their husbands. Sixty-five percent of women in senior management positions have children, according to a Families and Work Institute study. They kept their jobs and are raising their families.

We are seeing financial equality in the workforce, according to the 2010 United States Department of Labor Report, over 58% of all the women are the breadwinners and 78% of women are now in the workforce full time. *Yet this equality is not true equality,* as married women tend to have the lower-titled jobs lacking leadership and governing decisions, while men hold the CEO positions. There appears to be a shift in choice for women—work or family; however, that shift is on a false bottom as more women return to work after childbirth and more companies want them.

When we examine where women have been in the last decade, it is arguable we have not moved forward in leadership as we are hovering at 12.3% over that past decade for women on corporate boards (Warner, 2014). Is this due to a glass ceiling or a multi-reason effect? I thus argue before we scream Glass Ceiling...I can't get ahead because of the Glass Ceiling...we need to look a bit more. While 12.3% is a low number, the causation can be any for any reason. Leadership is a choice; more women choose to focus on family than work. Is this bad? No, because it's a choice.

Another factor is leadership skills—our leadership skills are different. I too have felt discriminated against due to my gender when seeking advancement; however, what I argue is that often when there is no ceiling in place, the phrase becomes a reason for lack of advancement versus that individual seeking out new skills to get you ahead. It is easier to blame a glass ceiling than to look inward and see your own truth that you may need a bit more development to advance. By stating the glass ceiling is in effect you are allowing your own needs to be overlooked. The accountability of yourself to be handed over to the organization verses you taking action. To that point, advancement is always a choice, and often a woman may not want the promotion as her desires may lie elsewhere.

Many women have been successful at breaking the glass ceiling only to find a layer of men.
Jane Harman, Former Congresswoman

WE NEED TO REDEFINE WHAT THE GLASS CEILING IS_____

Women in the business world often hear the term "Glass Ceiling," and while this is not a new phrase, redefining the glass ceiling is. Let me start by asking you one question: What has held you back all these years? Is it truly a glass ceiling, or your own lack of personal power or other skill sets to move forward? More to the point, does applying *quota attainment* in the business world for women in leadership work, or will this be another scapegoat as to where have all the good women gone? To that end, continuous attention to this effect only drives a larger gender gap in the workforce.

Men and women work differently, and men were there first, so they were the rule setters. If we were playing a game of *Survivor*, men already have in place the influence, communication style, and alliance in place to win. However, if you change your perspective of us versus them, you in effect change the playing field. Thus, redefining the glass ceiling to *the workplace mirror effect* may bring you a new vantage point on where you need to develop your own skills to get ahead. Focus on how you are doing your job versus how others are doing theirs. What skills do you need to improve? How do you communicate and negotiate? Look around at your peer group, borrow skills they demonstrate and strengthen what you bring to the table.

So what do you do if you feel you are in a glass ceiling environment?

I would be remiss if I ended this section here, as some of you are in a glass ceiling atmosphere, and yes some may have even created it. Now what? The simplest answer and one that has been stated several times in both women's leadership journals and *Harvard Business Review*, is to leave. If you are finding you just can't get ahead or are losing your drive to climb, move on.

You also need to ask yourself if the issue is you; harsh, I know. Yet often when women are in power, our communication can shift. We need to be respectful and apply solid communication solutions. It can be as simple as speaking with a co-worker about job performance behind closed doors, not in front of a group. Any leader needs to ensure her/his communication does not elicit an attack response (defensive tone). If someone in the workplace makes a comment that appears to be sexist, address it promptly. Be sure it is noted and have a conversation with that person in the company of either your direct supervisor or human resources. All too often the comment is made without thinking—not an excuse, just plain stupidity. By doing nothing, however, you are helping the ceiling grow.

Approach the workplace like the game of *Survivor* rather than from a gender angle. I am not saying play the game like a man, heck no. Play it with your own strengths and find new areas of development to work with.

Ask questions like:

- Who are your allies, and do they have the juice (influence) to get stuff done?
- Who do you eat lunch with? Your pals or those who can help you grow and get ahead?
- Have you defined your career path and let others know about it? Or are you waiting for them to guess what you want?
- Do you have the skills needed to advance, and if not, what are YOU doing about it?
- Who else around you has strong alliances? Can you merge yours with theirs, or are they opponents?
- In meetings, are you heard, or are you a wall flower?
- Do you understand the organizational power structure? If not, find out who does and then tap into that.
- Where do you network (your sandbox)? Is it effective?
- *Q-TIP: Quit Taking It Personally*! In business, it's business not personal. If it becomes personal, we are looking at a whole other horse to bet on.

The only thing you can change is yourself; meaning, if the organization truly has a glass ceiling in place, you have a choice: fight it or leave.

If you decided to stay, your second choice is how you fight it: gracefully or like a bull in a china shop. I recommend gracefully as the level of resistance towards you will be lower. Be clear and concise on what you want and what you bring to the table. Take bite-size steps to educate versus vomiting laws and statures. Pivot your viewpoint to that of an educator, not the enemy. Create initiatives and programs that address the issue and embrace both genders. Make it about leadership growth not gender neutrality, as their vantage point also needs to be taken into consideration, as well as the level of intransigence.

Shattering the glass ceiling can be confusing in today's business world as many believe there is nothing to shatter. How you accelerate at work is a direct reflection on you as a person. Be humble and climb.

Chapter 3

The Authentic YOU

With all the chatter on being authentic, what does it really mean to you, and who is the authentic you? Women have many roles in life; how can we be authentic to ourselves if we are playing other parts?

Defining Authenticity

I spent my twenties and thirties looking into the mirror and saw who people wanted me to be. I smashed that image in my forties and now I see the real me—and so does everyone else.

Recently, I was speaking with a group of wonderful and talented CEOs, and we hit upon the topic of authenticity both in leadership and as an individual. Is there such a thing as truly being authentic? Are we not copies of what we see and learn? Do we not judge each other by their cover or what we let others see of ourselves? Is truly being authentic a risk as we are allowing all to see who we truly are? What helps define that authenticity? Clothes, purses, and the car we drive or where we live? Then the questions continued as we explored the courage it takes to be authentic.

Simply put, authenticity is being in the mindset of honesty, truthfulness, and sincerity around our true self, our actions and intentions. It is being in the present of mind when making decisions.

It is the deeper understanding of why you respond or react the way you do, and moving beyond that to understanding your values and morals and how they impact not only yourself but those around you. It is keeping an open mind of how you were defined by others, the roles and rules that shaped you, and deciding if they, today, as in alignment with who you are today versus yesterday. This awareness also opens the door for continued growth as who our amazing authentic self is today will shift tomorrow.

And yes, from this definition it does sound easy, but there are two key ingredients required for authenticity. One is knowing oneself, and two, the hardest, is the courage to be oneself.

Authenticity is the collection of choices we have to make every day. It is about the choice to show up and be real, the choice to be honest. The choice to let our true selves be seen
Dr. Brene Brown

Authenticity does not just happen; it is a choice and a courageous one at that. One has to be willing to face all that she sees defining her and uncover the truth. The rules and roles, the past and present only shapes us, as it is ourselves that define us. It takes strength to then lead your own life with this conviction. Fortitude in one's truth is harder than living behind a mask and takes energy every day; however, in time this energy provides its own reward.

Know Oneself and the Masks We Wear

So who do you see when you look in the mirror? Is it a true reflection of you, or is it skewed with the vision of others or society? This is a very difficult question we need to ask ourselves. If we are not being true to ourselves, the next question I encourage to ask is what would happen if you were just you? How would others react? What is the worst thing that could happen? Are you happy as you are now, in a mask, or would you be happier out of a mask?

We all wear masks. They are a first line of defense when protecting our vulnerabilities and fears, and I am not saying we need to be naked and raw 24/7. However, the issue comes to be when the mask takes over—when we cannot uncover when we are wearing our masks and when we are not. Regardless of gender, this mask can take over one's life and can create unnecessary stress and health concerns. When a mask is in place for too long, our true needs in life may go unmet. It also takes a lot of work and stress keeping the mask intact. A mask is not a lie of who you are; instead it is shadows or shades of who you are.

An exercise I use with my clients on uncovering their true self is unmasking the mask, where you take some time and draw the mask you wear from time to time (on one side) and then on the flip you draw your true self. This can be in the form of words, photos, colors…this is your mask, so get creative with it. This can take weeks to do as what I am asking you to do is to uncover what the world sees of you and what the real you looks like. I suggest working with a coach to help you because the mask will try to "out-woman" you (you will like what the outer mask shows you so you can hide the inner you).

Once you create your mask, look and see how much true self and mask-self overlap. Identify areas of your true self you can now place out for all to see. Ask why you are hiding certain aspects of yourself; you may have valid reasons, but then again you may find some reactions just plum crazy. Slowly introduce yourself to the world. This takes courage. To neutralize the fear, write down the worst thing that could happen if you showed your real self.

Below is a photo of two masks; however, feel free to use whatever media you desire. Use the smiling face for the real you and the frown for the mask you show the world. Feel free to scan and e-mail your mask to me and we can chat if you would like more information.

THE BENEFITS OF AUTHENTICITY_____

Let's get right down to it: the benefits truly outweigh the risks of letting others see the real you. When you are living in your own self, without a mask, you will attract others who like you for you, not the persona. You are giving the best gift to all who love you: the gift of self. Your personal power increases, and restraints that held you down become apparent. You will achieve more of what you desire versus what you think you want. Stress levels drop, as you are no longer living in a false shell. When you are living in your own skin, the tangibles no longer define you. Other people who judge you no longer matter. Your comfort level in attire, style of car, purse, etc., will all reflect who you are.

Example: at the meeting I alluded to earlier, we looked at what our work image stated about our authenticity. The women at the table were all in senior executive positions in healthcare, and the vast majority believed they *had* to wear a neutral suit to work, almost as if not to be seen. One executive belief was that the higher up a woman rose, the drabber or conservative their suits had to be. Colors such as grey or navy with a neutral top or scarf become commonplace.

When I asked them why the color or lack of flair, the comment repeatedly fell to the desire not to draw negative attention to themselves. I then followed with the questions, were they happy with what they wore? How did it make them feel? How were they approached in the workplace? What did they wear outside the office? If appearance demonstrates the outer mask, how does their attire demonstrate their mask?

The end result of the conversation: all agreed their appearance did not reflect their true self—it was a mask or shield. To take it a bit further, one CEO shifted and embraced her fun-loving true self and began to wear fun colors. Her comment is below:

I noticed a change immediately in the energy level around me when I shifted into my true self and allowed others to see the real me. Not only did I connect on a deeper level with my co-workers, I also found a gained sense of trust and confidence. While I know it is not all about the clothing, the outer appearance helped me reveal the real me, to embrace me at work, take it or leave it. My overall job stress level also disappeared—it was as if the real me was dying to say Good-Bye Grey and Hello Workplace! – K. Piper CEO

Now by no means am I saying finding your style will increase your success. It will, however, shift you out of your comfort or hiding zone. Owning oneself is taking a risk with the greatest rewards. It is hard work, but dive on in—you are worth it.

We have to dare to be ourselves, however frightening or strange that self may prove to be.
May Sarton, Author

LEADERSHIP AUTHENTICITY

Let's go back to the earlier question: Can leadership be authentic? This debate has been argued quite heavily over the past several years with the results pointing toward a resounding YES. Organizations need authentic leaders. This leader has demonstrated an increase in production, job satisfaction and retention. It is based in learnable skills, but the difference in an authentic versus non-authentic leader is authentic takes personal authenticity first and foremost. Yes, we may have learned and embraced our leadership style by seeing and learning from our mentors, but authentic leadership involves taking those lessons and skills and making them yours. The biggest difference is that authentic leaders lead from their heart and the mind follows.

To define authentic leadership, I tend to agree with the majority of thought leaders that define this leadership by skill sets versus one true be-all definition. Authentic leaders tend to be real and know who they are, have a high level of self-awareness, and are focused and driven for not only their success but also the success of others. They are driven by organizational awareness and development. The focus is on doing rather than speaking in action. An authentic leader is a bouquet of integrity because it is whom she is, rather than whom she wishes she could be. An authentic leader never asks more of their peers than she would ask of herself. Her leadership style is part of her personality.

Have you ever worked with a leader who utilized intimidation as a form of leadership skills? Alternatively, one who was manipulative? These are not good leaders; they also are not authentic—unless that individual was a boorish manipulator 24/7. More than likely, they were copying behaviors seen by another poor leader.

Becoming an Authentic Leader

Self-awareness is the key to authentic leadership. Examine yourself and how you lead. Embrace the positive leadership skills you have and then mentor others in the workplace. This also helps you to create alliances for future utilization. Create a list of non-authentic behaviors—things you do in leadership because you have been told to do them.

Example: as a leader I was mandated to hold weekly conference calls with my direct reports. I hated these and found them to be useless. However, once I re-examined as to why and what my outcomes could be, suddenly I wanted to have these meetings, and voila—so did my team. I embraced the "task" but made it my own, focusing on what my team needed. Journal! Use a LEIP journal to note your behavior throughout the day, and then make adjustments where needed.

I've come to believe that each of us has a personal calling that's as unique as a fingerprint—and that the best way to succeed is to discover what you love and then find a way to offer it to others in the form of service, working hard, and allowing the energy of the universe to lead you.
Oprah Winfrey

You Have a Style

You already have an authentic style waiting to burst through, now let's identify it. Let us play a game used by many executive coaches. Below is a list of words. Write them down on sticky notes. Now grab a wall and sort the words by *Always Value, Often Value, Sometimes Value,* and *Not Important.* Rank each pile by highest value to lowest value. Here you will have a clear understanding of what is important to you and what is not. There is no right or wrong way to post your sticky notes, as this is all you. Now ask yourself, are you leading in your value system?

Accountable	Adventurous	Affluence	Amiable
Analytical	Authority	Balance	Calm
Challenge	Change Agent	Collaboration	Community
Competence	Competition	Conscientious	Confident
Courage	Creativity	Decisive	Developing Others
Direct	Diplomatic	Driven	Empowered
Enrichment	Enthusiastic	Family	Finance
Focused	Fun	Giving	Goal Orientated
Gregarious	Helping	High Standards	Humor
Influence	Integrity	Knowledge	Loyal
Patient	Personal Development	Recognition	Relaxed
Resilient	Responsibility	Risk Taking	Self-respect
Sincere	Spirituality	Status	Stable
Structured	Systematic	Task Oriented	Team Focused
Trusting	Understanding	Variety	Wisdom

There are several variations of this tool, so feel free to play with it. If you find some of your traits are missing, please feel free to add them to your sticky notes and send me an e-mail so too can add them to my deck. The beautiful part of this exercise, you can use this as a team builder or as I do using this with team values when uncovering conflict.

What is your Superpower?

While I would love to claim fame to this section, the idea of superpowers actually comes from Kathleen Burns Kingsbury, author and wealth psychology expert. A few years back, a group of us were sitting around at a conference when out of the clear blue Kathleen decided to give us all superpowers.

These are unique and special gifts that you have that make you special, the one thing that really makes you unique. It is what people remember the most about the authentic you. Kathleen has the unique ability to bridge two worlds together: financial and women, couples and wealth, speaker and bestselling author. I, on the other hand, create an atmosphere where you can just be you and be accepted, no matter what is happening. The best part about a superpower is while you shape it, others define it for you. It is how you are seen. Therefore, your superpower may change with the audience; as I am sure my kids would say, my superpower is "just being Mom."

So what is your superpower? It is what comes naturally to you. In fact, this is something you can do in your sleep. It is a set of skills that you have ingrained in who you are as part of your personal brand. I love to post this on Facebook and see what everyone notes.

Uncovering Your Hidden Gems

What do you think your powers are? Why do people come to you or are drawn to you? What do you solve in a single bound? What do your friends think your superpowers are? Do you like your power or do you want to shift it? This is a great conversation you can have with your co-workers, team members, and friends. It will amaze you how others see you. And once you know what your special powers are, you can use them to become more authentic to yourself.

Examples of Superpowers:

- Calm, cool, and collected under fire
- Fun-loving approach to stress
- Always being there, no matter what
- Selfless giver
- Can listen and process information in a single bound

Being authentic is the one leadership skill that is a gift to those you work with; it also will lead you to excellence!

Being the CEO of Your Life

Being a CEO of your life is the most rewarding career choice one can make, and you do not even have to interview, because the job is yours.

As women, we hold down a variety of roles; yet if we let these roles run our life, they can overpower us. Does this sound familiar, or have you ever made a list of all you do?

Meet Lauran Star (yes, me): I am a full-time, thriving business owner, accomplished author, international speaker, faculty member in the New Hampshire University System, mom of three, competitive girls youth lacrosse and soccer coach, boys youth soccer coach, mom of theater, baseball, and basketball, and wife of sixteen-plus years. In my off time I take on the role of doctor, cook, cleaner, peace keeper, homework goddess, dog walker, school volunteer, shopper, best friend, and supportive aunt to over twenty nieces and nephews.

The point is women wear many hats and can shift those hats at any given minute. Some do it seamlessly while others, well, let's just say they are overwhelmed. At the end of the day, while others desire to toss in the towel and sleep, I am left reminding myself that all of the above is my choice. I place all that on me. Why? Simply put, I am the CEO of my own life.

What does it mean to be the CEO of Your Life? In a nut shell, you are in charge of your own happiness both at work and home, and yes, it is a choice. I choose not to get overwhelmed by all the hats I wear; instead, I embrace my role and delegate as I need to. I understand when to say no and whom to turn to for help.

When I am stressed out I hold myself accountable to the reason why my stress level is high. I even have my own stress word. There are times mom just goes bombaloo – this is from an amazing children's book about managing stress and emotions by Sometimes I'm Bombaloo – by Rachael Veil, a must book if you have younger children. When I hit the wall, I let all know I am going bombaloo. It will pass however it does put my stress in perspective.

You can and should set your own limits and clearly articulate them. This takes courage, but it is also liberating and empowering, and often earns you new respect.

Rosalind Brewer,
President and CEO of Sam's Club, a division of Wal-Mart Stores Inc.

CEO of Your Life Job Description:

Being the CEO of your life is not waiting for success to happen—you make it happen!

JOB PURPOSE: The CEO of your life is responsible for providing fun leadership for themselves and the family by working with peers, family members, teachers, medical teams, and other work teams both inside and outside the home, to establish long-range goals, strategies, plans, policies, house rules, and happiness.

ESSENTIAL DUTIES AND RESPONSIBILITIES -Feel free to add your own take on being the CEO, as long as you are accountable to the task.

- Say no and delegate to those stronger in the vested areas of home and work.
- Plan, develop, organize, implement, direct, and evaluate budgets, time management, and personal health, ensuring all are met.
- Define what makes you happy and own it.
- Understand your own needs, as well as empower those around you to understand theirs as well.
- Give yourself permission to shift perspectives and courses throughout life to discover growth and uncover new needs.
- Define where the time losses are and strategically make ROI (Return on Investment) decisions.

- Be present in both home and work environments.
- Create a dynasty of individuals that you can turn to when in need of help.
- Understand who is eating your pie or energy (more in Chapter 6).
- Communicate effectively, using time-outs, breaks, and breathing.
- Ensure you are taking care of you—health, mental well-being, and downtime.
- Encourage your own personal development.
- Be held as your own personal accountability partner.
- Uncover others who can help you be accountable to yourself
- Keep a record/journal of all you do and how it makes you feel, then toss the bad and keep the good.

If you are looking at the list above and are thinking, I need to become my own CEO, go ahead and copy and paste these into your journal. This job description is not one size fits all. As your own CEO, you can now shape and shift how the role fits you.

It is time to start writing your own job description. Create a list of all the things/tasks you do in a day; keep a journal for an entire week. From there, identify what is truly CEO worthy and what you can delegate. Keep what is critical on your job description. This will help keep you focused on the end goals. Post this where you can see it daily as a reminder of what is important and what is not.

I like to post my delegation list on my fridge, as all good leaders inspire others to take on more responsibility. That list may include household tasks—dishes, laundry, and garbage— to parenting tasks: doctor/dentist appointments, after-school pick-ups, and volunteering.

Be sure to include a section on personal development. What or where do you wish to grow? This is a tough question that often we push off, but when we stop growing, we in plain text die. Look over past performance reviews; were there any skills in need of attention? How about your peers, can they share some insights? Personal development is not just for the workplace; maybe you wish to take up pottery or yoga, take a Spanish class or communications course. It could even be focusing on one's own health. My own development is in wine knowledge, which has nothing to do with work or family, as it has to do with a strong interest. I read wine books, attend classes and seminars, go to trade shows, learn about food pairing, and so much more. This augmentation is all about me. Set strong attainable goals, goals that are SMART: Specific,

Measurable, Achievable, Reliable, and Timely. While SMART is not a new method of defining goals it came to be the gold standard in **November 1981 issue of** *Management Review* **contained a paper by George T. Doran.** Be careful you do not set yourself up for self-sabotage by selecting goals that are unrealistic, e.g., losing 200 pounds in the next six months. Dig in deep here as you are the most important expense in this job description.

Uncover an accountability partner, someone who will be there for you and yet can hold a mirror up to you so you can see clearly. I have several close friends who do this for me daily. These are the friends who have no issue asking, "What the hell are you thinking, girlfriend?" They are in my corner 24/7 no matter what.

If you find you are not in a position to have this co-creative relationship in the corporate world, then you may need to go and hire an outstanding coach. One who is perfect for YOU. Hiring a coach/mentor can be challenging and time consuming. Ask around and see who others use rather than throw a dart at the World Wide Web for a name.

Recently, I was interviewed for a section of *No Winner Got There Without a Coach*, an anthology put together by ISBN publishing. Below is what I had shared regarding hiring a coach.

QUESTIONS TO ASK YOUR PROSPECTIVE COACH_____

Who is your ideal client?

It is imperative that the coach you select know his or her ideal clients or the kind of person they will only work with.

My answer is simple: I work with women who are very take-charge; they are open, honest, and not afraid of the tough questions or the tough action steps that we are going to discuss or put forth. They take accountability and are willing to make mistakes. They are willing to take risks and understand the benefits of coaching, fully knowing it will take energy and time for success.

In understanding who I am and whom I click with personality wise, I know right away if we will work well together when we have the initial consult.

Example: if the client immediately starts placing blame elsewhere, this is not going to be a client I am going to work with.

What is your coaching style?

The coach should also know their style of coaching, and this style needs to meet yours. If you want someone who will let you cry for an hour—if that is what you need—find a coaching style that provides that.

I am very direct, and very forward. I am going to call it as I see it. I am going to make you think and work hard. I will ask those questions that will make you uncomfortable. However, realize that being uncomfortable in a co-creative relationship allows for personal growth. I will never judge you. I am your strategic thinking partner concerned with all of your needs.

What are your credentials?

This is critical because coaching has become a catch-all for a variety of fields. Look for degrees, experience, certified coach training, work history, and thought leadership in the field with which you need assistance or that at least match yours.

I have fifteen years of leadership experience with several Fortune 500 companies. I have my master's degree in Industrial Organizational Psychology. I am the founder of Lauran Star Consulting LLC where our focus is on Leadership Development/Diversity and Empowerment. I am a certified executive coach, as well as licensed in several assessment tools focused on development.

Ask your potential coach for success examples. How does he or she see success? How would your potential coach address a situation you're facing? Ask them for a referral to another coach. If they are well plugged into the coaching community, they will have one.

Below are questions you need to ask yourself when evaluating a coach after the initial consultation:

- Can you be open and honest with your coach?
- Do you feel safe and not judged with that coach?
- Does that coach have enough credentials behind him or her, or enough academic learning to be mentally stimulating, as well as your thinking partner?
- Then, putting all of that together, does their personality jive with yours?

If, in the end, something does not gel with who you are, move on. I could be the number one coach in the entire universe but not right for you. Again, it comes down to that personal connection. You just have to click with your coach.

Being the CEO of your life is also a mindset. It is the belief that you have a choice. *I do not have to pick the kids up today from school—I choose to.* It is an internal desire to grow and be the best you can be. Yes, being the CEO of your own life comes down to your own personal accountability to yourself. You are in the driver's seat...now drive.

Lead Your Ship
Women's Leadership

Leadership is not management—it is empowering others to reach new heights, motivate, and shift ideas for the greater good of the company or oneself.

Leadership is a choice, and not for the faint at heart. It is hard work, yet the rewards are unmeasurable. Leadership is your sweet spot, if it gives you goose bumps. Some argue great leaders are born and yet others state leadership is learnable. Regardless, we all have a natural affinity towards a leadership style, be it transformational or transactional. It is part of our basic personality. Great leaders are authentic and true to themselves first. They hold themselves accountable before all others. They act with integrity and trust. Inspiration of greatness can then only follow. The style of leadership is a leader method—their individual vision is their approach.

So, are leaders born or created? I argue a dash of both as leadership is a choice, a need and desire, beyond just wanting, at least for great leadership. Understanding leadership is the first step in finding your own style.

In the millennial business forum, great leadership is a must for any organization to thrive. Companies are pivoting from transactional leadership (otherwise known as managerial leadership) toward transformational leadership, and it is no wonder why. In the early 80s to late 90s, managerial leadership worked because business growth was focused purely on transactions, rewards and punishment. Even our political atmosphere of the past encouraged transactional leadership, however today it is transformational leadership. The vast difference between leadership and management is the getting there. Management focuses on the needs to get done with minimal organizational change, whereas leadership is about understanding how and what to change to improve the infrastructure.

Today's business structure is driven by the success and needs of others as we enter a business realm of constant empowerment. Effective leadership is placing her self-gain after the net gain of an individual or organization because her gain is that gain. Due to technology changes, communication assets are critical to great leaders today. They need to be reliant on every means available to them to share their message and have an input. Today's employees want to feel included in the greater cause. There are more women in the workforce and they are driving the economy. The modern business structure is more transformational or encompassing of the whole rather than of individual actions.

True leaders understand that leadership is not about them but about those they serve. It is not about exalting themselves but about lifting others up.
Sheri L. Dew

TWO KEY LEADERSHIP STYLES AND BEHAVIORAL TRAITS

To understand leadership, we need to explore the two key styles at play today in the business world. Okay ladies, this is your warning as I am about to geek out on you.

Transformational leadership: I defined this a bit early in the book, but let's dive back into the water. *It is the ability to lead through understanding all parameters of the problem and taking into account the needs of all individuals that the change encompasses. It is having superior vision to guide change, to inspire and motivate others toward greatness. This leader is trustworthy and ethical, a role model to all and one who empowers others to take ownership of their work. They are not without fault, but are flexible enough to overcome shortcoming and embrace accountability. They are big-picture leaders and feel there is no box.*

There is a high level of emotional intelligence and productivity which results in lower employee turnover, greater job satisfaction, and more effectiveness associated with this leadership style. According to Lopez-Zafra, Esther, Rocio

Garcia-Retamero, and M. P. Martos (2012), Business Emotional Intelligence is the adaptive interaction between emotion and cognition that includes the ability to perceive, assimilate, understand, and handle one's own emotions and detect/interpret the emotions of others. Transformational leaders have this tenfold and are always working to improve their skills. It is said transformational leadership raises awareness at the individual level—raising awareness of the importance of the organization's goals; thus, individuals rise above their own needs for the organization's success.

Transformational leadership is an overall effect the leader has upon its followers, which is to say they are leaders who are admired, trusted, and respected. These leaders can connect with their team and can impose the self-concept of organizational visions within the organization (as cited in Reuvers et al., 2008), thus lending themselves toward strong Emotional Intelligence scores (Goleman et al., 2002).

A glance at Transformational Leadership:

- **Adult Learner:** Ongoing life learning and both professional and personal development is part of this leader's mantra. It also provides new pathways and tools for her to empower those she works with. An internal ability to help others see things differently and solve issues or problems with a new lens. This behavior is focused on ongoing pivoting of problems and outcomes.

- **Accountable:** She is accountable to herself first, then to others. She does not take this lightly. Transformational leadership is all about raising the bar higher and higher, and then reaching it herself.

- **Change Driven:** Goes hand in hand with proactive action as both are needed for organizational success. While they may not love change, they certainly embrace it. They see opportunities before they become problems and begin creating a plan of action.

- **Individual consideration (Bass 2008):** The focus of individual attention to all, especially those who have shortcomings. They are in your corner when you need them. Employee gain is a focus.

- **Intrinsic/Inspirational motivation (Bass, 2008):** Simply put, clearly describing the expectations and inspiring all to reach those goals. They also establish those expectations based on each individual need and are enthusiastic and supportive around you reaching those goals.

- **Idealized influence (Bass 2008):** Speaks to doing as I do, not as I say. Establishing strong values, ethics and integrity, and then leading by example.

- **Pro-Active:** They see and understand what needs to change in the company, as well as how to get it done. They do not wait to be asked to solve an issue; they already have identified and have begun strategizing the solution.
- **Results Focused:** In the end, results are expected and understood.
- **Vision:** Vision is a critical behavior for this tone of leadership as innovation and inspiration are boundless.

Transactional Leadership: This style focuses on the role of supervision, organization, and group performance. Its leaders reward follow-through based on both rewards and punishments. Leaders using the transactional approach are not looking to change the future; they are looking to merely keep things the same. This approach is focused on working for the institution and the boundaries that are pre-established. They love the status quo and strive to maintain it.

A glance at Transactional Leadership:
- **Compliant:** As this method is also known as managerial leadership, they tend to be more followers. They thrive when working within the culture's substructure.

- **Extrinsic Motivating**: Motivation is based on external rewards such as money, trips, and cash. One reward tends to fit the entire group.

- **Hates Change**: Change is never seen as a positive; however, they can help change happen by being given specific tasks.

- **Organizational Goal Setting:** As opposed to transformational, this character is focused on the organization first, the individual second. Goals are set accordingly. The reward is then given when said goal is met.

- **Pragmatic:** This is how they tend to solve problems.

- **Reactive/Responsive**: This dimension focus on the reactivity of an individual when problems arise. They tend to be those managers who are constantly putting out fires or are waiting for the next one.

- **Self-Interest**: This mode of leadership is driven by self-interest and thus motivates from that frame work. The end goal is theirs and the company's—not the team's.

Today's leadership demands resiliency in the ever-changing economy. It has the bounce-back appeal with a bit of *Tigger* tied to it. If we think back to our childhood favorite Tigger had the unique ability to bounce back no matter what the circumstance required. It is not seeing the market with rose colored glasses, but rather seeing the truth and areas of change at face value. Leaders excel in accountability and understanding their own vulnerabilities; therefore they work tirelessly to build upon their strengths and to fortify their weaknesses. They understand their blind spots and adjust their mirrors so as not to be blindsided.

So where does gender fit in to these two styles?

There are some differences, but no one gender is better than the other.

It is not unpredictable that leadership style began shifting in the millennial decade as employer-employee dynamics began to shift. Today, we have more women in the workforce. Women tend to be more extroverted and intuitive when addressing issues or problems (Brandt, Tiina, & Laiho 2013). Additionally, women are the main consumers in the United States and hold the purse strings—leadership had to pivot.

Women and Transformational Leadership

According to Uma & Glenice (2006), women in western culture tended to lead with transformational leadership, whereas men tended to be more transactional. Remember, a leadership style is a method that can change. At the time of these studies, the business climate was based on the transactional model. That being said, the authors go on to note women leaders tended to be more democratic and participative, meaning they tended to be non-dictators, delegating and egalitarian. They found men were more direct and delegating, but their approach was based more on transactional leadership. Silverthorne (2005) also noted on the difference of gender in leadership: men and women demonstrate drive, charisma, teamwork, determination, ambition, and strive for success at equal levels.

Project GLOBE's work, extensively examines leadership roles throughout the world and concludes women of western culture have a strong affinity towards transformational leadership in large part due to our Emotional Intelligence skills set. House et al. of Project GLOBE further examined, from a global viewpoint, where genders differed. The data demonstrated women again tend to be more democratic and empathetic which are both Emotional Intelligence Competencies.

EMOTIONAL INTELLIGENCE COMPETENCIES

Emotional Intelligence and Leadership: I would be culpable if I did not include a section here on Emotional Intelligence and its role in leadership. To be a great leader, you must have strong Emotional Intelligence.

Emotional Intelligence (EI) is the study of how individuals relate to themselves, as well as to their peers both in and out of the work structure. It is the ability of self-awareness, as well as awareness of others in the emotional concepts. It then focuses on how we manage that relationship (Goleman 2006). It is also confirmed by Goleman's work that Intelligence Quotient is responsible for 10% of an individual's success compared to Emotional Quotient of 80%. The study of Emotional Intelligence and leadership is not a new concept, as Orioli Cooper and Bar-On were the first in the field, Bar-On coining the name *Emotional Quotient* in the 1940s. However, EI became widely accepted in 1996 with the work done in the field by Danielle Goleman.

Lichtenstein & Plowman (2009) reviewed the need to improve the overall dynamic interactions with all individuals within a workplace environment, thus improving overall leadership skill regardless of gender and Emotional Intelligence level. They found those with higher Emotional Intelligence scores under leadership were perceived more positively by their employees/peers.

Leadership Styles and Emotional Intelligence

There is a plethora of data supporting the use of Emotional Intelligence to improve leadership styles. In reviewing the research on transformational leadership styles, regardless of gender, all cases demonstrate favorable results when Emotional Intelligence training is added (Brown et al., 2006). Mandell and Pherwani (2003) take it a step further by researching the effects of gender; they found there are some areas men will score higher than women and vice versa, but the overall scores tend to be closely related. This also rang true for leadership styles, as those who were considered strong leaders scored relatively high in overall Emotional Intelligence.

Mandell and Pherwani suggest Emotional Intelligence training and coaching for all leaders. They also suggest Emotional Intelligence scores may assist organizations in hiring tomorrow's leaders. This is in congruence with Danielle Goleman's (2002, 2006) and Laura Belsten's (2006) work on Emotional Intelligence and defining strong leaders. However, Mandell and Pherwani believe strongly that differentiating the gender strengths is an area that requires more focus.

In understanding Emotional Intelligence, it is also understood that when reviewing competencies, men and women will score differently. Yet on a whole, there is not a gender difference (Goleman, 2006). Mandell and Pherwani (2003) state there are differences based on gender and thus overall improvement by bridging the gender gap, as well as collectively adapting leadership style. Duncan (2007) reviews gender-specific competencies and finds that although women tend to excel in the categories of empathy, social responsibilities and creativity, they also score high in other more male-dominated areas such as vision and change.

Although Goleman (2002; 2006) states there is no gender bias in Emotional Quotient, meaning no one sex does better than the other as a whole, there are slight differences regarding the competencies. Women and men are on equal standing when reviewing Emotional Intelligence, but in this literature review I have taken the next step to see if there is evidence that shows the two genders are equal when focused on two of the critical components for leadership success: visionary leadership and catalyst for change (Goleman, 2002; 2006; Belsten, 2006).

So what does all this mean in regards to women and leadership?

Leadership skills are learnable. We—regardless of gender—can adapt and pivot skills to our strengths regardless if you are transformational or transactional based. In the 1990s, I learned my leadership style from men. In the United States Army, the leadership style that is more acceptable and result driven for the organization is transactional. Therefore, my style took on a transactional appearance. Even though I had an inclination towards transformational tendencies, I adjusted and pivoted my assets in the direction of transactional leadership, and in the business world then, it suited me well. In the wake of an emerging transformational style, I again pivoted and embraced my natural propensity towards that form of leadership.

The age-old question of gender in leadership needs to stop. We should focus our attention on the skills.

I argue gender does not matter! Both genders can be equally wonderful or lousy at leadership. It all comes down to how you pivot your skills, what you allow yourself to be open to learn, and how you inspire others to move forward. Leadership is both born and learned. Leadership is a passionate choice. No matter the level of your skills in leadership, if the passion and desire to lead is missing you lack the drive to succeed. You can have the best transformational training, but without the excitement or goose bumps to activate yourself, those skills are better spent training others who are.

Presenting leadership as a list of carefully defined qualities (like strategic, analytical, and performance-oriented) no longer holds. Instead, true leadership stems from individuality that is honestly and sometimes imperfectly expressed....
Leaders should strive for authenticity over perfection.

Sheryl Sandberg,
Author: *Lean In: Women, Work, and the Will to Lead* COO
Facebook

While Sheryl and I come from very different backgrounds and our perceptions of the world for women are somewhat different, we both agree leadership demands authenticity. As women, we need to stop looking around and comparing ourselves with others. Instead, look inside yourself and see what makes you who you are. Look to see where you lead successfully and embrace that energy. Bring that forth in other areas of your life. Be open to ask for information and help.

Ladies, remove the pride and embarrassment around lacking knowledge—we all have to learn somewhere. Shift your thoughts towards being a sponge; like a child, take it all in—look at what works and what does not, what feels natural and what makes you cringe. Write it down in a journal; it only takes a few seconds to make a quick note. Empower yourself to grow.

I was once coined La La Q/A while employed with Johnson & Johnson. I always started a question with a question such as, "Can I ask you a question... Do you have a moment to brainstorm with me ... May I get your opinion?" If I did not understand something I asked, especially around the motivation of action. I am a kinesthetic learner, meaning I am very tactile when it comes to new processes. This technique comes through questions. I also was never told to never ask.

This is how my male counterparts learned procedures, and thus it worked for them and me. I learned how to gain my money in my paycheck by asking a co-worker how he negotiated. Ta-da, now I have that skill. I would watch closely in conflict to find new methods for resolution, what worked and failed. Make notes and move forward.

Here is the beautiful and powerful statement: post it somewhere you can see it daily.

There may be thousands of amazing leaders, but NO ONE leads like YOU do.
You are unique, you are powerful, and you lead because it is YOUR choice to do so.

SHIFTING PARADIGMS: LEAD YOUR SHIP_____

So how do we now go from all this knowledge and skill to leading our own ship? It takes visionary leadership to get you moving forward. You need to have a plan and then attack it. The best part of visionary leadership is it works both at home and in the boardroom.

Visionary leadership involves moving yourself and your business to the next level by bringing the decision-making process to the forefront. These leaders are inspiring, innovative agents of change, creating strategic plans for a better tomorrow. They understand the full impact of all decisions made and moving in a direction of positive fulfillment (Star, 2012).

Have you ever asked yourself:

- What does leadership look like to me?
- What makes a great leader?
- What do I have in common with great leaders?
- Why do I want to lead?

Followed the above with:

- Are you motivating, compelling, and inspiring?
- What is your vision for your life?
- Can you tactfully challenge the status quo?
- Do you create a common goal and purpose for your team or company?
- Do others feel they belong to something bigger when they are with you?
- Do you think inside or outside the box?
- Do you have your own vision in place?

What I have noted in working with thousands of leaders: A GREAT LEADER is constantly changing and evaluating their strengths and areas of development. They are never stagnant when it comes to personal and professional growth. They never see black and white, as they think in grey.

Create your own vision and action steps to achieve it. I love using my vision board for this and honestly adjust it every six months. It is a colorful and creative way to uncover your personal vision and engage the "'why" in relation to your own authenticity and leadership. If you would like more information on Vision Boarding, you need to reach out to Steve Gamlin of *Inspired by Steve* (http://www.stevegamlin.com). This is my vision board as of today. It is posted on the wall directly in front of me in a frame. I see this every day to remind me of my vision for life. What does your look like?

Lauran Star

Chapter 4

Identifying your Needs then Versus Now

As your life changes, so do your needs. Why do we then ignore or refuse to re-assess or hide them, I wonder....

Needs are for Survival—Wants Make Life Interesting

*Often what we want is not what we need.
Needs are for survival and happiness; wants make life more interesting.*

First, you need to understand your needs.

When was the last time you sat down and asked yourself: What are my needs? Surprisingly, we are very good at placing everyone's needs well before our own, and then we are shocked when we can't create a list of needs for ourselves. We are also often confused about the difference between a need and a want.

Needs are things, both tangible and non-tangible, that we must have to survive. Needs get us through life with fulfillment and purpose. They motivate us to strive and succeed. They help shape how we see our world and are forever shifting or changing. Our basic needs are food, shelter, water, love, touch. Think of those as your core needs. Our needs also come in many shapes and sizes. Personal and professional needs may share some similarities but often are entirely separate.

Personal needs are love, respect and intimacy, while professional needs may be mental stimulation, financial freedom and recognition.

Wants, on the other hand, are things we like and that make life a bit more fun. Examples: fancy cars, designer clothes, big homes, sparkling gems, and a wine cellar to die for. While we may need a car to get to and from work, a want is the style or level or status that the car brings you. Wants are often the tangibles that help us uncover the why or the need.

The Boardroom versus the Bedroom:

The Boardroom represents your career and the Bedroom represents your home life. In many cases, our needs overlap both such as the need for respect and acceptance. Then there are the basic outliers in needs that are at opposite sides of the pendulum. The need for love and physical connections comes from the bedroom, whereas the need for financial solvency lies in the boardroom. It is imperative we understand and give ourselves the permission to recognize the work/life paradigm in the undertaking of understanding our needs.

Our needs often shift or change as we age. Think back to your twenties—what did you need and what did you want? Was your need in the Boardroom for work recognition, through the desire to climb the corporate ladder? In the Bedroom, women have a strong emotional need to feel loved, and while need is apparent at all ages, the need to procreate is ingrained in our hormonal DNA. We will be exploring and examining the difference in the boardroom and bedroom, as well as how our needs shift in the next few pages.

When we understand the difference between needs versus wants, we then can clearly identify those needs, and life fulfillment can happen. If we are lost in what our needs are, we are never truly happy, no matter how many *things* we have. Things only provide a Band-Aid to your need.

Here is the kicker: if you don't understand what you need from work or home, you can find yourself often conflicted about being happy. You will not be able to negotiate your salary, or say no to roles, set boundaries, or be present for the best moments of life. If you cannot uncover what your needs are, how can you expect them to be fulfilled. I personally recommend a needs check both personally and professional every year—and yes, write it down. Uncovering your needs, your true needs, does not take place over night. This again is work (seems to be the ongoing theme in this book), as you need to be completely honest and selfish with yourself. I give you permission to put yourself first.

SHIFTING PARADIGMS

Can you list five (5) personal and five (5) professional needs? Now ask yourself, how will you get these needs met? What do you need to achieve your need? What are the barriers in place stopping you?

Once you identify your needs, ask yourself:

- What is in the way of your achieving your needs?
- Have you shared your needs with anyone? What was their response?
- In the past, where did you achieve your needs? How did you do it?
- Who can help you along the way? Gender does not matter.

In this chapter we will explore both the boardroom and bedroom and where your needs may lie. By breaking down each need, you will create a clear needs pathway to achievement.

The Bedroom: Sanctuary or Laundry Room

This is my sanctuary, my space at home where I can just be me. A place I can connect with my kids through hugs and kisses, where I can connect with myself through reading or meditation. This is NOT where I store laundry—it is my sanctuary.

When you look at your bedroom, what do you see? Is it a place of harmony or chaos? Is this where laundry gets stored and then sorted? Is it busy or peaceful? Of all the rooms in the house, as women and men, we tend to neglect our bedroom. It is the last room we clean, where we hide stuff when company is coming over, and where we tend to store the stuff in our lives that no one else gets to see. The humorous side of the bedroom, however, is we tend to spend six to eight hours if not more in that one room. We find sleep there, where our bodies and minds rest and repair. We find companionship and comfort, love and warmth in the same space when loved ones are around. So why do we ignore this room?

My theory: our bedroom represents our home life. Stay with me here and see the similarities of your bedroom to your home life. Does your home life resemble your bedroom? Make a list of your home life, the pros and cons. Is it cluttered with too many outside obligations? Is it fun loving with a sense of ease and approachability? Can you see any dust, or is it compulsively clean? Do you laugh in your bedroom and life and thus use the home life to escape? Is your home life lived in, or is it a showpiece? Do you have rooms and furniture that are saved only for special occasions? Are there places in your home life where you stash junk away from prying eyes for fear of judgment? Is your home life your sanctuary? Do you know what your home life needs to meet your own needs, or is it all for show? Is it full or empty of personal belongings? Now look at your bedroom...do you see the connection?

As women, we tend to hide a bit in our home life; we allow others to see what we want them to see. I have acquaintances who define themselves by the car they drive, the number of friends they have (even if those friends are just energy suckers), how big their house is and how often the cleaning people come. This is living in your wants, NOT needs.

Yes, these women are acquaintances, not friends, in large part because I value **quality over quantity**. The best gift a friend can give me is to just be herself. There is no judgment here. If you understand your home life needs, authenticity and better friendships as well as lower stress will follow. These are true friendships based on you, not who else you hang out with. If you are living outside your needs, have you ever asked yourself what would happen if you allowed yourself to embrace what your needs were and be true to yourself?

Our Ever Shifting Needs

Our personal needs rotate as we age. When we are children, our basic needs are food, shelter, water, health, and love. As we mature, those needs still exist, but we add to them. In our twenties, women often find themselves looking for a mate or life partner. The need to be loved and have physical connection is hardwired into our brain. It is part of the Maslow Hierarchy of needs platform. However, if you do an online search on "what women need," you will find: furniture, executive demands, car advertisements and more. In other words there is no easy definition of what a woman's need are either at work or at home. It is no wonder we are confused over what we need at home and what we want. When we try to identify our needs, even the so-called experts and bloggers do not get it right.

So let us really take a look at needs—basic needs every woman has—and examine how they shift as we mature. Notwithstanding, this list is not comprehensive, as needs are personal. I examined the needs most of us have.

WOMEN'S HEALTH

Good health is a NEED not a want. In our early years, our twenties and thirties, we tend to take our health for granted. Sure, we go to the usually checkups, maybe hit the gym, eat whatever we want, stay up late, etc. However, when we hit late thirties and forties our health starts to become a priority as things start to break. We find ourselves aching in places that never ached, we need glasses, our breast health is now a larger concern as well as all female parts, etc. However, I do have to argue, why do we wait so long to focus on our bodies and how well they function? Why are we not focused on this from day one? And, the bigger question: who is in charge of your personal health? Is it you or your doctor?

In order to be in good health, you have to know what is under the hood. You have to examine your own family history and then ensure your practitioner is 100 percent in tune with your needs. Simply put, you have to take accountability of yourself and your well-being. As women, we are so good at putting all others' needs in front of our own. We say things like, "I will get to that later," "I'll lose the 20 pounds next month," and "It's only a small bump," and then we are shocked when it becomes serious.

First, look at who takes care of your health from a medical perspective. Can you be 100 percent open and honest with them? Are they proactive in your care? Do they let managed care rule them or your medical needs? Do you feel any judgment from them around your habits or do they empower you to find solutions? Are they in-the-box thinkers or out of the box? If you found yourself going *hmmmmm*, you may need a new doctor. I am extremely fortunate to have two outstanding women, who happen to be physicians, helping me attain this need. I can be myself in the office and share everything surrounding my physical and mental health concerns.

When I turned forty, my primary care physician, Victoria Blight A.P.R.N., saved my life. She decided with my family history of colon-rectal cancer it would be wise for me to go in and have a baseline colonoscopy. There was a little push back from my insurance as I was only forty and the history affected males in my family, yet Vicky pushed on. During the exam, two aggressive pre-cancerous polyps were discovered. Had I waited until fifty— well, let us just say I would never have seen fifty. Now beyond feeling lighter that day, I am also wiser. I do not take my colon health for granted. I focus on a high fiber diet and every two years lose a few pounds in three days.

You have a choice for your medical well-being: ignore it and hope for the best, or take action and ensure the best outcomes regardless of what life throws at you.

To Be Heard and Seen

Not surprisingly, this is a need versus a want—as again this falls under Maslow's Hierarchy of Needs. Acceptance is critical to anyone's overall health and prosperity. It is also one of the top complaints successful women have about home life. They feel they are not really seen or heard at home.

Unfortunately, society helps set the stage for women to be seen and NOT heard. I grew up hearing this from my own mother. Girls in school even today get the message to be a pretty girl, a nice girl, let the boys win, it is okay if you struggle in math, you're a girl, and so much more. Even the media perpetuate this. Look at female politicians—how often do they get blow back on a comment that if a man made it would be fine? I know more about who dresses Michelle Obama than her personal political platform, and Hillary Clinton is pegged negatively because we do know her political platform—and her hairstyle is either in or out. This sends a message to all of us: be seen, not heard.

What do we do, as women, when comments surrounding appearance cloud the real message? Do we stand up and say ENOUGH, or do we chime in? If we want to be heard, then speak up. If not, we complain when we are not heard.

Wouldn't it be easy to just shout out how you feel? It takes a bit more finessing and boardroom tactics to be truly heard. Emotional Intelligence is critical surrounding being heard. The focus on keeping your own emotions under control while stating your vantage point, as well as how you communicate, are all learnable skills. While influence and power plays may not be as important in the bedroom, ensuring you are heard is.

Checking in to ensure what you said is understood. Being sure the messages behind the comments are understood goes a long way. We dive deeply into this in the Boardroom, and the best part: you can use those killer skills here too.

You Time

When was the last time you took time for you? What fuels your passion? When you are not working, do you take time to play, or is it family time only? What gives you cake? Often we forget we need time to decompress, process, or just breathe in order to function at a high level. This time may be spent at a yoga or fitness class, reading a good book, a bubble bath, or just going to the movies alone. The last movie I saw in the theater was a kids' flick...I like to call this time self-love. Do you journal or meditate? There are plenty of ways to get you time. The best kept secret is: it can be in five-minute increments. That's right, you can meditate for five minute or journal, take a few deep breaths and focus, and even reading a bit of a great book is you time.

When I hear women complain they barely have enough time to run to the bathroom let alone go work out at the gym, I have to ask, and whose fault is that? Wait for it...it is your fault. You see, you have to want to have time to have time. One reason women are at a loss for time is that we tend to say yes to everything. I am now in the habit of always checking my schedule before I say yes. I also look over the return on investment for time. In other words, I never make a decision regarding my time on the spot. I always weigh the outcomes in my schedule. If I can take on the volunteering spot without giving up me time then I do, otherwise it's a NO.

Saying no is easy, once you know how. I, like you, struggled with saying no. I would even go to the extreme where there was no time for me and then still say yes. So how did I learn? I have a no list. I have a list of five to ten reasons to say no and how to say it.

It looks like this

"Gee, I would love to step up and _____, but I have been hogging all the volunteering spots this year and it is unfair to the other moms. So I have to say no."

"At this time, my schedule is full. I just cannot fit another thing in."

"If I had more time to move things around…but not at this time."

"I already give to the Make-A-Wish Foundation—this is my family's charity of choice."

"I need to check my schedule, but I am thinking it's a no."

Create your own list. Judging from my list in the bedroom, can you see what gets asked of me? My boardroom list is slightly different. I love stepping up and volunteering—heck, I coach youth sports every season. However, I select what I am saying yes to with a keen eye on protecting my "me time."

Healthy Relationships

Humans need to be loved. This is not a want, it is a must. How that love comes about is through healthy relationships. Your partner/spouse, children, and close friends all create solid connections for you to thrive in. Finding these relationships takes hard work. It is also scary as you need to be in your authentic self to attract authentic friends and relationships that last.

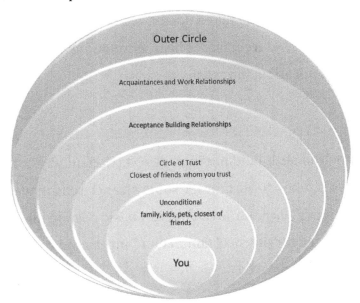

As women, we tend to struggle with where people fit in our life. Do all your friendships provide you with needs attainments, meaning do they all give you what you need in the form of the relationship, or is it fluff leaving you wondering? I like to think about my relationship in circles with me in the center. The first ring is filled with people who love you unconditionally. The second ring includes those people who also love you and have your back; this is the circle of trust. The third ring is friendships along the way that could become second ring, or acceptance building. The fourth ring is acquaintances and work relationships; here, trust is on the line.

In doing this either mentally, as I do, or on paper, I know where my relationships stand at all times. It also provides some protection from being taken advantage of or having too high of expectations. A large part of healthy relationships is based on communication and trust.

THE BARE FACTS OF THE BEDROOM AND PHYSICAL NEEDS___

I would be remiss if I did not include a section on physical intimacy—yes, a taboo topic that for some strange reason we are afraid to breach with our loved ones. A basic need in all humans is the need for physical contact and intimacy. Women need to feel sexually desired.

This section is NOT the end-all-be-all for your sexual questions. That is another book and for an expert like Diana Hoppe, M.D., author of *Healthy Sex Drive, Healthy You* to address. The funny thing is men are not mind readers. If we are to have physical relations that are successful, we need to be able to share what our basic sexual needs and wants are. This is not just a female issue, as men too struggle with sharing their basic urges and needs.

So let's begin with re-iterating the health benefits of sex. Sexual relations or intimate physical contact, that is, correct intimate contact such as cuddling, kissing, and holding hands, increase overall well-being, decrease stress, increase your immune system, and so much more. When our physical needs are met, our cortical steroid levels are low. This is the steroid that helps regulate stress, insulin, body fat, immune response, and overall well-being. Physical contact, of course, is not the only way to decrease this steroid, but it sure is fun.

To understand how our sexual needs and wants shift over the years, we must first examine the hormones that help regulate our urges. I will focus on the three big ones.

Oxytocin is released during orgasm and is responsible for the connection feeling; it is one of the "bonding" hormones both men and women share.

Estrogen's function regulates our sexual desires—it helps get us in the mood. So when we are young and our body is ripe with estrogen, women tend to be a bit more sexually active. The same happens at or around forty as our bodies begin to prepare for menopause. There is a drop in hormones before menopause, irregular cycles, and a roller coaster of hormones with peri-menopause. As we mature, we become a bit more comfortable with our own body; thus we tend to be a bit more adventurist—if we allow ourselves.

Testosterone, while plentiful in our 20s, begins to plummet in our 40s. Testosterone's function is around sex drive. It is not uncommon to hear women in their 50s note the lack of sex drive. However, keep in mind cuddling, kissing, and holding hands can still fill a physical need.

Vitality in the bedroom begins with one's own health. I strongly encourage you to speak with your physician about the changes in your body, what you like and where you are struggling. Download a complimentary copy of *Hormone Therapy—the Pendulum Swing—Finding the Right Balance* by Diana Hoppe M.D., http://www.drdianahoppe.com/perimenopausal-menopause/ to understand what is going on and what can be done about it. You need to be in charge of your female health.

There are some factors that also come into play in the bedroom surrounding why both men and women find themselves at a sexual loss. Some of those factors include medical, psychological, and socio-cultural issues and often are diagnosable when the right questions are asked. The relationship itself also may change. It is often said, and my husband would certainly agree, I am not the same person he married. Thank God for that, as I have grown and matured, and so has he. Life can get in the way, and so can kids. Energy levels drop as the day moves forward. Our physical attraction or communication may push us in other directions. Sexual confidence may also come into play as our wants may change as we age.

Our needs in the bedroom also change. By a show of hands, how many of you have faked an orgasm? Do not be embarrassed, as you are not alone. According to Brian Alexander (2014) of MSNBC, well over 80% of women fake orgasms on a regular basis. We all have faked it a time or two…or three, and no wonder—we are tired, need "me time," may feel uncomfortable with our bodies and so forth. However, here is where it bites us in the end. We are responsible for our own orgasms, not your partner. Let me say that again: *to orgasm or not is your choice*—your partner is there only to assist you along. If we are faking it, how is our partner supposed to learn what we like or need?

The hormonal shifts and sexual factors affect men and women equally. The key to understanding these curves in the road is to discuss them. Every six months or so, I pick up a copy of *Men's Health*. This magazine is full of men's issues my husband does not like to share. I even let him read it. On the flip side I also pick up a copy of *Women's Health* for him to read. The best part of this is that it provides a starting point for conversations. It gets the hard dialogue moving forward. It also helps focus on where the true issues are and stops the blaming game. No longer are we pointing the finger at each other for not having our sexual needs met, now we understand a bit more around the why and taking accountability.

So how do we get started?

- Get comfortable with your own body, understand what works and then share that. Ladies, if you are not comfortable with your own self, how can you expect your partner to be?
- Take care of yourself; exercise and eat right. Get enough sleep. I am not spouting anything new here, as I am sure any self-help book you have read on sex states the same.

- Have quarterly sex meetings—I know it sounds hokey, but it works. Set up a time to meet with your partner to talk about sex. What works, what does not, and remember, do not use the word YOU. Also talk with WE (see Chapter 5: Communication for more information).
- Read to each other. If you are uncomfortable with the vocabulary around sex, pick up a good book like the *Kama Sutra* and read and discuss the photos. Giggle and have fun.
- While I am not a fan of setting up sex dates, it is important that we take care of our needs. Find some alone time with your partner—hey isn't that why our kids have playdates?
- Follow others who can offer up advice and information. Diana Hoppe, M.D. is certainly a gem to read and follow, as well as "Dr. Jenn" Gunsaullus, Ph.D., of www.drJennsDen.com.

In the end, a healthy physical connection takes work on both sides. It takes open dialogue around what is working and what is not in the bedroom. Leave the judgment at the door and be open and honest with each other. If you desire something, share it.

Pivotal Woman

Diana Hoppe, M.D. Author of *Healthy Sex Drive, Healthy You*.

How can women empower their own sexual desires?

First, you need to look at where and what your desires are. Be honest with yourself and make a choice; if you want more and if so then go after it. Put it in your schedule and let yourself have that time. Even scheduled sex time can be full of fun and spontaneity. Wear something sexy or flirty. Encourage your man to step up and help you find your sexual desire. Let him know together you both can have a wonderful and exciting sex life. Share what turns you on or allows the mood to happen—this can be as sexy as putting the kids to bed for you so you can get in the mood or running a bath and a glass of wine. It's the small things that spice up your relationship.

OUTSIDE THE BEDROOM WALLS

So what about the rest of your needs at home? As I stated earlier, the bedroom can be looked at as a direct reflection of your home life, so where else are you struggling? Can you list your top five needs at home? And the bigger question is—how will you get them met? Often once we uncover what our needs are, the obstacles preventing those needs rear their ugly heads. Identify where those issues are and how YOU will get around them, and you will be moving forward.

Wearing Heels in the Boardroom

Just because I am the CEO does not mean I am no longer a woman.

I separate out the boardroom and bedroom in this section because often what works at home does not work in your career, but the reverse is not true. You will find what is working in your career can also be applied in the bedroom or home life. One reason is due to the nature of self-awareness in the office. We also tend to be less driven by emotions at work than at home. Women in the workforce tend to also be mission oriented. We are there to get stuff done so we can go home and enjoy the fruits of our labor.

Why Women Work

In order to understand our needs in the boardroom, we must embrace why we are there and what the tone of our career looks like. When women entered the workforce decades ago, the landscape was masculine by design, but today that landscape is changing dramatically, and organizations are struggling to keep up. The reasons women enter the workforce also fluctuate and range from the need for financial gains to the need to feel accomplished.

Think back to college or high school; what did you want to be when you grew up? Me, I wanted to use theater to help kids' process trauma. This was my dream career, but due to funding—well, college had to come second to eating. I worked full time while in college, as well as joined the United States Army as a paramedic to help defray the cost. Did it work out in the end? Twenty years ago I would have said not really, but today—absolutely. Sure, I received my degree, but the degree I received had to be modified to fit my workload.

The point being, my career aspirations in my twenties were very different to where I am today. In my twenties, post college, I went into sales; why? Simply put, I needed money to pay back all the debt. I stayed and excelled in sales leadership for sixteen years, climbing the corporate ladder, never seeing a glass ceiling, and even getting fired a time or two. My leadership work focused in the healthcare arena, and while I prevailed, I was not thriving. I was working. My needs were not truly being met. However the journey I took to get to my needs being met fostered the authentic Lauran to surface.

The military showed me there were no boundaries to what I could aspire to. That men and women could work together side by side and climb together. I would be a fool to say there was true equality – however what I learned was equality was in the eyes of the beholder. If I wanted it bad enough it could be gotten. I just had to figure out a way to attain it. Furthermore going into sales and leadership my psychology degree began to stretch itself as I became quickly adapt to understanding both people and organizations needs and desires. To that point I discovered when I place it all of my past strengths together voila I rocked it.

Today, after looking even harder at myself I have found my sweet spot. I am internally motivated to inspire and empower others; it is a driving need. In consulting, speaking or writing, this motivation/need gives me goose bumps. I call this GBE: the Goose Bump Effect. When I was leading teams in the corporate world, I would flourish when others shined. However, this was a very small part of my workload. It took me twenty years to understand my GBE and how to achieve it, as well as build a business around that need.

WHAT MOTIVATES YOU TO GO TO WORK_____

Interestingly, the GenYs/Millennials are all over this; they know what motivates them as they are focused more on having a positive input and outcome on employment versus just working. They watched us as they grew up, seeing and hearing how we like or did not like our jobs. When my children ask me why I am working, I let them know without any hesitation it is because it gives me the GBE, and I want that for them. We must understand why we have a need to work—what cup does it fill? The best part: one answer does not fit all, because we are all individuals.

Motivation falls into two categories: internal and external, and we can have a dash of each. Internal motivation is your heart in your career. It is the desire to do something because it is enjoyable. Praise is not needed, as you feel completed by the task itself. Examples: being part of another's growth, writing a book or dancing because you enjoy it, or diving into an area of development out of curiosity.

External motivation is a result of rewards and punishment. They do something because it gives them a tangible prize. If you are thinking *this sounds transactional*, you are spot on. In the sales arena, the vast majority of salespeople are externally motivated. However, your motivation can shift as you mature and the tangibles may lose their shine. This is one reason we find employees stuck in the same job that once was fulfilling yet today is not. They do not understand their motivation has changed.

In understanding what motivates you to work, you can then develop career plans that ensure your motivational needs get met. Share this with your employer, ask for development in this area, and seek additional opportunities to shine here. Then dig a bit more and see what other needs you have.

Top Four Workplace Needs_____

Being Heard. Just as in the home life, women have a need to be heard in the office. This takes a bit of personal power.

Personal Power: the ability to get what you desire in a tactful way. It is the overall ability to assert yourself in any situation and then maneuver the situation into a win/win resolution for all involved. It also is a visible and visceral, strong inner calm. It is the inner belief that you are in charge of your life and can accomplish anything you want, if you want it badly enough. It also is the ability to let go of those things you cannot control or wish not to control. I believe we are all born with personal power. It is full accountability to what you are saying and why. (LEIP Forward! Gaining Emotional Intelligence: Tools for Today's Woman Leader, 2012)

Emotional Intelligence is the key to being heard. Now you may or may not know, Emotional Intelligence (EI) is how we relate to ourselves and others. It drives success in the workplace as 10% of what makes you successful is brain power; the rest is EI (Goleman, 2009). The best part is that EI is learnable, and personal power is a proficiency of EI.

As women, we tend to quickly give away our power, both in meetings and in recognition. We must understand it is a good thing to keep our power, to speak up in meetings when issues arise, to allow recognition to flow and to learn how to say thank you and smile. The other aspect of being heard is communication.

Communication is the ability to pass along information in a manner that is clearly understood by the audience. It is presented through verbal, written, tone, inflection, and body language skills. Sounds easy, right? Wrong! This is probably the trickiest area for women and men, as tone and inflection are part of communication. Because men and women communicate very differently, the message can be confusing or even become lost. Let's face it, no matter the gender, some folks do not have a clue about how to communicate effectively. It is easy enough to misunderstand an in-person communication. Now that e-mail communication has become so prevalent, the potential for misinterpretation and harm is so much greater. Texting, blogging, and tweeting are other forms of communication all with a different subset of rules and vocabulary. (As if English does not have enough rules.) (LEIP Forward! Gaining Emotional Intelligence: Tools for Today's Woman Leader, 2012)

It's not what you say but how you say it.

People can easily hear a smile in your voice and a smile is the universal language of friendliness and the greatest predictor of your likability.

Mary-Ellen Drummond

Being Heard

Be sure you have a plan with key points that need to be made and addressed. Leave emotions out of the conversation. Be careful when using the word "you" as this insinuates blame. Be clear and concise, and ensure your body language is approachable. Give yourself permission to breathe first—then comment. Speak when you wish to be heard and not just to speak. Take personal power of what you are saying and be flexible when ideas need to shift. Listen…listen…listen… take notes when others are speaking to ensure you understand correctly. Be present in communication, meaning have your head in the game or keep your mouth shut. If there is a misunderstanding that is fine—just acknowledge the misunderstanding.

Unfortunately if you feel you are not being heard, it is your developmental issue, not theirs. Take a course in communication and/or hire a coach to help you grow here. The only one who can address this is you, not your listener.

Being Seen

What do you wear in the boardroom? Are you dressed in greys and dark blues with a comfortable pair of shoes? Do you wear old undergarments under the scrubs you put on? How does your attitude shift when you dress for power? Are you colorful or dull? Is your work attire more like a uniform? Are you causal or formal? How high do you button your blazer and shirt? What does your jewelry say about you? How about your hair: modern or do you have the old-fashioned twist up? To bob or not, short and sassy, streaked or framed?

Believe it or not, all of the above says a TON about you. You have a need to be seen and accepted at work, but is what you are wearing truly you or your shield to keep all away? If you truly are interested in being seen versus being the wallflower, the first step is embracing who you are, not what you think others want to see. Think about the questions above. Did some of them stir you to think, "I wish"? How people see you is all a projection of what you want them to see.

When working in the corporate world, I was amazed at the lack of style. I understood the need to be business first in style, but that does not mean dull. I would wear my suit—never grey or black mind you (I look good in gem colors)—and always had a flair for fun. It could be as simple as a fun piece of jewelry, something that reminded me of me, not of who they wanted me to be.

I had a colleague ask me once why others saw her as the office monitor, meaning not approachable. Her wardrobe was a grey suit, white shirt buttoned to the top, pearl earrings, light makeup, and a hair style my mother wore in the 70s. Her outer appearance screamed: DO NOT APPROACH. Yet this woman was one of the funniest people I have ever known. When I brought to her attention her attire, she commented, "This is what business dress is supposed to look like." If you are not comfortable in the skin you put on in the morning, people can tell.

Relax ladies, I know you are thinking beauty is only skin deep, and I am suggesting you're judged by what you wear. However, one needs to recognize the truth for what it is: of course you are judge by what you wear. We are a visual society. What I am truly saying is, if you wish to truly be seen, then wear or dress in your true skin. It does not have to be a major shift. If you like wearing your hair in a twist and your personality screams fun, add some fun bling to the twist.

More to the point, what we wear shapes our attitudes. When you are going out with your friends on a Friday night, what do you wear? Something fun and flirtatious or comfortable jeans? Does not what you throw on set your mood? Why not do the same for work? In my undergrad I worked in a hospital setting; therefore my attire was scrubs. You can bet I had on fancy lace underneath. It was a wonderful reminder that I was still a woman even in that ugly, baggy, blue uniform. In attending my son's Boy Scout meetings, as an assistant leader I wear the official Boy Scouts of America uniform...with a dash of pink underneath and a fun coral color pin on the collar. I may be a leader, but I am still me. You know this is coming—if you want to be seen, show yourself.

Saying No

Women struggle more at work than at home with saying no. The rationale behind the difficulty is that if we say no today, there won't be an opportunity tomorrow. As I noted in the bedroom section, saying no is a skill set. First you need to empower yourself to see your schedule or tasks as yours. They deserve all the attention you can give them. Ask yourself, what is the return on investment if I take on this additional task or responsibility? What will I learn from it, or am I just taking on someone else's work? Taking on extra obligations can be part of your developmental process and may help you advance; then again it may not. You need to understand the full scope of the duty before saying yes.

Positive ways to say no in the company need to be clearly defined to reason, meaning you cannot say no just to say no. If a project comes across your desk that is not developing you or has zero return on the time investment for you or the company, then be prepared to hand it off to another. As a CEO of my own company, I have a list of skills and areas of development for my entire staff or team. When a project comes along, I ensure it goes to the individual who has the most to gain from the experience. As a leader, you yourself can do the same. Know who works around you and who is looking to advance. Create a list of responses or the go-to no list that you can pull out when needed.

Some responses may be:

I would love to do this, but _____ is looking to grow in this area; maybe we should give her the opportunity to fly.

I can do this if the turnaround time is two months out, but otherwise we will need to find someone who has the following skills to take this on.

What is the end result you are looking for? Why not challenge _____ to take this on her plate.

In saying no from time to time you allow the opportunity to develop others. Pivot your perspective to see the positive in no versus the negative. Trust me, when you say no to the right stuff and allow others to shine, you too reap the rewards.

Professional Development

Imagine a time where organizations were responsible for your professional development. For some, this was the reality we came from. For others, it's urban legend. In the past decade, organizational-focused professional development has faded into the sunset as employers now leave the development up to you. It is your responsibility to figure out what skills you need to work on and how you will achieve aptitude in those areas lacking. The management is there to help fund these endeavors and support you when they can, but the burden falls on you. This is also the case when human resources becomes the duty officer in your advancement. They are there to help you find opportunities, but ultimately it is your gain to grow.

Good, bad or indifferent, professional development is not a want, it is a need, especially if you plan on advancing or joining another company. So how do you develop yourself? Here is one of the few exceptions where you need help. You need someone who can show you where you are lacking or falling short. A mentor or advancement specialist—someone who knows assessments as well as how to coach growth. You may find this person in human resources, but keep in mind human resources works for the organization, not you. More often than not, you may have better luck outside the company. Look for someone who works from a hybrid coaching/mentoring model. This is a professional methodology that enhances your strengths to achieve your goals. As a result, work and life will be improved on your terms. While coaching is not a new field, very few are true hybrids with the extensive business background that can also mentor you up the ladder. You should be looking for a thinking partner to create a synergistic or co-creative relationship with you for your goals.

Research about hybrid coaching (Star, 2012):

- A proven way to improve executive leadership and organizational performance!
- Executive women and leaders enrolled in coaching found an overall improvement in their work/life harmony.
- Those who were coached had a better understanding of how to approach gender decisions and issues.
- Leaders and executives who were coached created a better relationship with their peers and their direct supervisors.
- Individuals who were coached exceeded their personal and professional goals.
- Hybrid coaching develops strong organizational leaders and executives.
- Women executives and leaders who are coached achieve their goals faster than those who are not coached.

Utilize your performance appraisals to your benefit. Ask the questions: where do I need to improve, what skill do I need to advance to, if there was one area to work on what would it be, and who can help me? In the end, if you wish to advance you must develop yourself. If you wait for someone else to do it for you, you will miss the opportunity of a lifetime.

Chapter 5

Balance the Misnomer: Work/Life Strategies

If you are happy at home, you are more likely to be happy at work and vice versa.
Thus the flip is also true…
If you are unhappy at work it will trickle into your home life, and you will be more likely to be unhappy there as well.

Lauran Star

Balance the Misnomer

Click your heels three times and repeat after me: There is no such thing as balance, so please, stop chasing it.

The statement is not too shocking when you think of the amount of time we spend in both places and the interaction we have with each other. According to the Corporate Executive Board (2011), only 23% of employees noted they had a positive work/life relationship. **That equates to 77% of organizational leadership not finding harmony with work and home life.**

For years, authors, coaches and experts on work-life harmony have been talking about finding a balance for work and life. However, balance is a misnomer in large part because there is a vast difference in work and life roles. We do not spend equal time at both places, have equal or similar roles, responsibilities and support to name a few inequalities. *At work you may be the leader and at home you may be the follower.*

While we are seeing financial equality in the workforce—according to the 2010 United States Department of Labor over 58% of the women of duel households are the breadwinners and 78% of women are now in the workforce full time—it is imperative both men and women learn work/life strategies together in order to succeed.

Organizations equally focused on work/life solutions as the Return on Investment (ROI) in being happy and fulfilled at home and work equates to Organizational:

- Increased Productivity
- Increased Health and Attitude
- Decreased Turnover
- Increased Retention
- Improved Job Satisfaction
- Decreased Stress

Just to name a few...

LIFE WHEEL ACTIVITY

Have you ever done a life wheel activity? This is where we look at your life as a whole and where you are playing. Below is an example of a life wheel. It separates out work, family, and relationship with partner, friendships, and more. The point is, we need all of these in our life. The wheel itself does not show work as being equal to home time. The boardroom is only a sliver of the wheel. On the wheel below, mark out your level of satisfaction with each area. Zero (0) being center and no satisfaction and ten (10) equaling the greatest satisfaction. What did you notice? Where do you need to focus more attention? Did the results surprise you? Feel free to change the table titles if there are things in your life such as Spiritual or Civic duties and activities. This is your wheel and where you spend your time will be different than others.

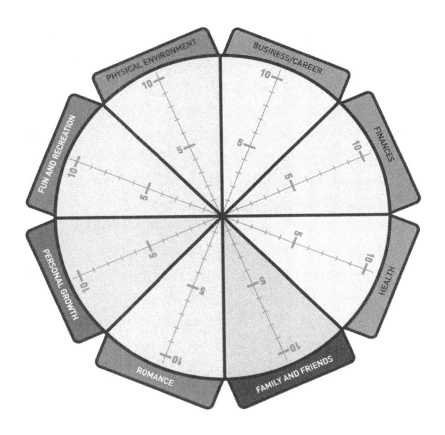

So, where do you need to build strategies? Often if you take boardroom strengths and apply them to your home life—notice I said apply not *dominate*—solutions will find you. Home is much like a boardroom in that critical decisions are made and financial goals are set. Success is dependent on many factors that are both people and things related of which we have little control over. Strategies are meant to be shared not kept secret; they help build strong teams and a united vision and goals both at home and at work. They also can be utilized everywhere! So dive in and learn some new strategies and find work/home harmony.

Communication Strategies
Stop Emotional Sabotage

Once blame comes into play, our brains shut off and all semblance of normalcy is gone.

How do you communicate at work versus at home? Is there a difference, and if so, why? What are the end results in both places? Some further questions to consider:

- Do you let emotions lead, or are you more likely to lead with structure and fact?
- Is it collaboration or one-sided?
- Are there clear and concise skills?
- Do you listen?
- Take notes?
- Set agendas?
- Set goals for the communication?
- Select the best time to have an emotionally-charged conversation?
- Set time aside to communicate?

All too often when we are at home, and sometimes at work, we allow our emotions to rule our conversations. Now I am not saying emotions are bad, but they can sabotage your conversation quickly as blame typically follows. Keep your emotions under control when communicating is not an easy task. I am a very passionate person, thus it is far too easy for my passion on a topic to overrule the message.

The art of communication is quickly becoming a lost skill as social media is slowly taking over. The lines of work and home are now non-existent when it comes to communication as most of us are reachable 24/7 thanks to those gadgets called cell phones. Texting information is quickly becoming commonplace, as well as finding important personal information of Facebook. Does this sound familiar? I have a client who was notified her grandmother passed in a Facebook comment. Recently I was notified of a medical update regarding my loved one via Facebook then followed with a text.

Relationships with loved ones are falling into the gaps. Children (the youth) are quick to text messages and not share (verbally) emotions, issues, and fears. Spouses and partners are struggling to find time together, thus leaving all to uncover and understand the nonverbal cues. Nonverbal cues are very confusing as you need to understand the other's personality to clearly gain insight on the cue.

While I believe it needs not be said...apparently I am one of few. Social media is a marketing tool as well as an informational highway. That being said, all too often people are now using social media as a means to get uncomfortable information to each other.

So please readers, **do not encourage the following Social Media behaviors.**

- Posting death or marriage notifications until everyone has been notified either in person or by phone call.
- Arguments: I don't care if you're fighting with your spouse, partner or BFF.
- Health issues of anyone until everyone again is notified via phone call or in person.
- Nasty, look-who-I-got-to-have-lunch-with, rub-it-in-your-face posts. (I un-friend these people.)
- Anything that will make your mother blush.

We all need to remember in this technological world that once it is out there, it's out there and you are judged on its content. What you post is a direct reflection of who you are. If you post propaganda and it is incorrect, you look like an ass. Trust me, I unfriend more people for the crap they place on SM than I keep. Then again, when I am bored I tend to play and tighten the screws with those who get all riled up on the pages. Thankfully, I live a very busy life.

Organizations also are finding communicational generation gaps as often Generation Y and Generation X are at a loss as to how to share information effectively. Add to that, studies show only 7% of communication is verbal, leaving 93% nonverbal; it is no wonder emotions and other distractions are sabotaging your communication. Where does this leave social media and texting in communication if the 7% verbal also equates to written?

To find effective strategies in communication, we must first start with communication awareness: How do you communicate and how would you like to communicate? How are you perceived by business partners, colleagues, spouses, life partners, and family? Are they hearing what you are saying or are you saying something different? Understanding how you are perceived is also a significant issue in today's interactions; one only has the first seven seconds to make a good impression in person or via social media and/or texting.

Can we take emotions out of conversations all together? No, as they provide a huge learning application and interpretation. The risk: when we ask others for feedback or express concerns, needs and desires, emotions often bubble to the surface.

Emotions open the door for blame and confusion. They also play a large role in nonverbal communication. If 93% of what you are saying is nonverbal, and nonverbal demonstrates emotions, it is no wonder emotions can sabotage. Emotions such as passion, anger, sadness and excitement can overtake the conversation, shifting from the message to the emotion.

The kicker to communication strategies: they work! They

are equally effective in the boardroom and the bedroom. When strong communication skills are in place at home harmony cannot help but follow. It is at home were we see the first gains in improved communication, in large part due to our need to lead with emotions at home. When you are not in work mode you tend to allow your heart to lead in conversations. As I noted before emotions can sabotage the best of intentions in communication, thus when you dive into communication with this awareness at home you will see the results almost immediately. We also see an increase in overall conflict resolution when these skills are acquired. However, remember it takes time and practice.

VERBAL COMMUNICATION STRATEGIES

Focus on we and us versus you and I.

In successful conversations in the boardroom, we often state "What is the solution **we** need? Or what do **we** need to do to ensure success?" We also are clear and concise with our questions, thoughts and comments, leaving emotions out of the conversation. Utilize the same skillset at home. "How do **we** save money? How can **we** find more time together? Where are **we** struggling? What do we need to do to get there?"

In taking the "I or you" and replacing it with "we or us," you refocus and take blame away. You also become included in the conversation versus dictating the conversation. If you could imagine an emotional balloon, using we instead of I deflates the balloon. This is also a wonderful tool if you have children as often they feel "attacked" in communication.

Understand how the other person communicates

Believe it or not, we all do not communicate the same way. Understanding how the other communicates is simple to do. One needs to listen first and understand the others communication style. When one understands the other person's communication style, we can effectively communicate.

Below is the Everything DiSC® diagram (Graph 1). In the simplest of terms, when communicating with another person, are they assertive? High assertion equates to a D or I personality, low to a C or S. Then ask: Is the person task oriented? This will give you a general sense as to how they communicate. I will dive in a bit deeper in a moment, but if you truly want to see where you fall and understand how Everything DiSC® can work for you, please feel free to shoot me an e-mail at Lauran@LauranStar.com and we can get you set up for an assessment and debriefing (please note there is a fee associated with this; however, the end results are amazing).

Graph 1: Everything DiSC®

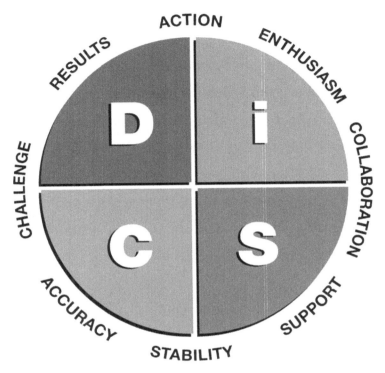

I am very assertive and love people; yes, you guessed it—I am "I." Where do you fall?

Styles of Communication: There are several wonderful books out there on how to communicate with DiSC, and I encourage you to read them as this is just a dollop of information on communication.

D: Directors are direct and to the point—they like information without drama. They want to know how the end results look. D's lead with facts.

I: Inspirational people...well, it is all about them—how does this affect them? They love a good story, the more details the better, and make it fun. I's lead with emotion.

C: Conscious people are number and task oriented—they want just the facts, nothing else. They are analytical and enjoy making lists. C's lead with lists.

S: Steady people are concerned with how the outcome affects others, and they prefer as many details as possible. S's lead with people.

Here is where it all comes together: I am a high I, which means I love good stories, details, fun, and yes, please make it relevant to me. My husband is an engineer and a C, thus he tends to be very analytical in both communication and life. When we get into conversations, I have to remind myself...facts first, emotions last. That means I need to adjust how I approach the issue at hand and remove the emotional tone out. Otherwise we get nowhere. On the flip side, my husband has to remember I lead with emotions first and he needs to listen to me from his emotional brain to understand what I am trying to communicate. It is a give and take.

Define and share your needs both in the boardroom and the bedroom.

Organizations, teams and/or partners cannot read your mind—you need to open up and share what you need verbally. However, emotions can sabotage stating your needs...

When was the last time you shared your *needs* (not wants) with your employer? When did you sit down with your boss and share where you wish to go developmentally? Keep in mind, your business development is YOUR responsibility. Did you write it out, follow up after with an e-mail bullet-pointing the main thoughts? What emotions did you feel when you wrote out your needs plan? Did you write them down and get them out of your head, or did you bring them with you to the conversation?

The same questions can be asked in the bedroom. Do you know what your needs are at home? All too often women forgo their home life needs and become the heartbeat of the family, yet they allow the mind to drift. Do you need you time? Who are your friends—do you see them? What needs do you have for fulfillment? Do you keep all this to yourself or share it?

By writing it all down beforehand, you can edit your emotional responses and provide a stronger argument. You also will appear more confident and prepared as the nonverbal cue such as confidence, your posture, eye contact, is re-enforced in the writing your thoughts down. You purge the negative emotions on paper, not the person. In the end, it may help you get what you need.

Set communication agendas both at work and at home

In the boardroom, we set appointments and have agendas for all our meetings (or you should). This will keep everyone on track and in the know. Agenda's should be clear and succinct, allowing time to include prospecting of other issues.

In the bedroom, as crazy as this sounds, if important conversations have an agenda and time frame, the results are often positive. Yes, make an appointment with your partner/spouse when having a conversation on money, goals, needs, and anything else that is important. Then create an agenda of what you want to discuss, the pros and cons and what the needs may be (money, time, etc.). Write it all down and then give it to the other person so they can review. This also allows you to see any emotional triggers so you can deflate them before the conversation. Keep the agenda clear and concise. During the meeting, take notes, and after, create a follow up. Being the CEO of your life requires a bit of work and management.

No one likes to be caught off guard in a meeting both in the boardroom or bedroom.

Journal before and after emotionally-charged meetings

Journaling is a wonderful way to purge unpleasant thoughts, say things you wish you said and make comments to grow from next time. Keep two journals a Bedroom and a Boardroom Journal.

BEDROOM JOURNAL

Journal, journal, and journal: this activates the RAS (Reticular Activating System) in the brain and helps you wash out the real emotions versus the knee-jerk ones. It will help you keep life in perspective. More to the point, journaling will keep you focused and on track in the home life.

Take five minutes before and after emotionally-charged conversations to write things down. What were the triggers, what do you regret saying, what do you wish you said. If you know you are going into an emotionally-charged conversation, write down how you are feeling, get it all out before the meeting; this will clear the emotional garbage away.

Let your partner/spouse know you are journaling. Encourage them to do the same. This will allow them to also keep emotions from ruling the conversation and keep them on task so they don't say things they regret later.

I love to journal late at night; this is a longer session as I may write down fears, concerns, and dreams. This writing is all for me and keeps my mind clear when I sleep. A journal can be a to-do list for your dreams. Feel free to share or not—this is your journal.

BOARDROOM JOURNAL_____

Business journaling should only take about five minutes per session. That is unless you are writing down your goals and career plans, which will take longer and should be written out and reviewed every six months.

Before every meeting, write down what YOU need from the meeting, what you need to keep in mind and who the triggers are in the meeting. Create quick solutions for how you will deal with those individuals who push your buttons in the meeting. You guessed it: you are creating a game plan, and in writing it down, you create a pattern of success.

After the meeting, write down what went well and what did not. Focus on how you should have responded or reacted. This will get it off your mind and create a path for next time. This is also an excellent tip for those heated encounters where you get stumped for words or action. Write down what happened and what you would have liked the reaction to have been.

Regardless of the journal type, writing down your positive and negative responses and actions clears your mind and prepares you for next time.

If you know you are a poor listener or struggle being present in conversations, keep a notebook with you when you are having a lengthy conversation with your friends, partner, spouse and co-workers.

Write down what appears to be important, and then ask for clarification at the end. "So, if I heard you correctly, you need x, y, and z, is that correct?" Listening skills are a learned behavior, and, like a muscle, if you do not use them you lose them. Writing it down will also help you keep present as you are actively engaged in the conversation.

We all have heard, seen or taken a listening class at one point in your career, and one thing is for sure: not much has changed. You must listen, think, and then respond. All too often we respond first, then think and listen. Yet what we are responding to tends not to be the true issue that is being communicated. This is purely emotional or knee-jerking to what is said.

How to improve listening:
- Read and Practice the art of active listening.
- Know your communication style.
- Take notes when the person is speaking, instead of processing what has been said.

- Allow gaps in the conversation. Do not feel the need to fill those holes with words.
- Don't interrupt.
- Be focused on the other person—do not multitask. Take notes as a means to keep engaged.

Remember the **Three T's:** *Timing, Temperature, and Tone*
Often it is not what you say but how you say it. Keep your tone soft, with proper inflections, thus keeping the interest of your listeners.

Timing: Is it a good time for *this* conversation? If not, set it aside and schedule a time. Hint: As you are walking into a crazy house, it is not the time to discuss the level of noise.

Temperature: What is the general mood for the conversation? If you are in a bad mood, is that really the way you want to discuss finances with a loved one?

Tone: This is indicative of the emotional charge in the air. If you are angry, they will hear it. Take a breath and remove yourself from the situation or conversation. It is always okay to say, "I need to take ten before continuing. Can we pick this up later?" Don't let tone ruin your hard work.

Strategy for Nonverbal Communication_____

The best strategy for nonverbal communication is self-awareness. This involves being aware of how you are standing, if you are present, what your face is doing, and what your hands are doing.

In my marriage, I was unaware that when my husband wanted to discuss money, my face said it all. I cringed and my left eye twitched. It set the emotional tone for the conversation. Even if the discussion was positive, we felt the negative effects of my body language. Finally, he mentioned my expression. I then had to dig a bit deeper inside myself to understand why I responded this way—understand it and then move away from it.

Self-awareness is not an easy task. It takes time to understand why you respond the way you do and then to address it. However, this skill set will definitely set you apart both at home and work as self-awareness helps you see what is important and how to regulate your actions. My favorite work in this arena is *Self-Awareness* by Allan Twain. This is a wonderful workbook focused on this skill set.

Change takes time. Be patient with yourself, your partner, and co-workers if they too are working on communication. If they are not, you might want to say to them, "We need to work on our communication style so we can reduce any conflicts."

Resilience Strategies
The Tigger Effect

Resilience is the ability to change, adapt, and improve with the times. It is the ability to see an issue and its solution using a positive dynamic. It is the bounce-back factor, or "Tigger Approach." It is being empowered about the end results regardless of what the situation is. It also is being realistic and optimistic about the future.

In today's work/life structure it is more important than ever to be resilient in your work and life. So many things are changing, and at such a fast pace! If you are not resilient, you may be left behind. I would be remiss to not mention that in communication, resilience is critical.

Being resilient both at home and work means being flexible to changes and not letting them get you down. It is a forward motion in life regardless of the changes. However, the boardroom demands resilience; if you are lacking this skill you could lose your job. It's no wonder when you place workplace resiliency in a search engine, a plethora of information comes to light, as organizational resiliency results in positive job performance, a reduction in stress, and overall improved job satisfaction.

In the bedroom, however, resiliency tends to get left at the door. For some strange reason, of which I have yet to discover, women who are high on the scale of resiliency at work leave it there; they come home and then struggle when schedules, meals, or childcare goes ballistic. Women often think we should be able to go home and have life the way we want it, yet forget the skills needed. Maybe we are too tired or unfocused.

However, there is hope, as society is slowly adopting the flexibility needed to create harmony. The days of June and Ward Cleaver are over as we see in shows like *The Middle* and *Modern Family,* where the focus is on diversity and bouncing back. The best news: the skills at work apply at home. So in thinking of one of my favorite childhood characters, Tigger, resiliency is all about bouncing back.

Life is not about how fast you can run or how high you can climb but how well you bounce.
Vivian Komori

So HOW DO WE BUILD RESILIENCE_____

Challenge yourself to change

The first step to increasing your Tigger Effect is to be aware of changes that need to be made. What do you need to improve upon to create harmony at home...or at work? Where are you struggling? What have you seen work and not work?

One tip in seeing the gaps is to surround yourself with people who are resilient and ask for their help or awareness. Many times we are not even aware that we are in failure or non-resilient mode. Create a support system. Make a list of people who are resilient and can be your support system when you or your plan falters. When you suffer a setback, create a list of steps to take to get out of it. If you are stuck, then ask for help from your more resilient friends and co-workers.

Find a theme song

So I will admit it: I love the 80s and 90s and was a fan of *Ally McBeal,* a 1990s sitcom. She had an episode where the dancing baby created a theme song for her, and yes it stuck. I explore this technique myself and with my clients. Guess what...it works.

Multiple studies demonstrate music stimulates the brain and emotional responses often in the positive. Music tends to lighten your mood and elevate your spirit. Find a song like Chumbawamba's "Tub-thumping" or Tom Petty's "I Won't Back Down." Look at Katy Perry's "Firework," Destiny's Child's "Independent Woman," or Alicia Keys's "A Woman's Worth." Find theme songs that are specific to your life, then download the song to your desktop, iPad, and cell phone. You may be surprised how quickly this will make you smile and help you bounce back. Make it personal.

Q-TIP: Quit Taking It Personally!

Believe it or not, it is not all about you. Regardless of where you are, we often believe it is all about us when in fact it is not. Stop and think…maybe your partner just had a bad day, and your reaction will either make it better or worse. Same goes in the office.

As women, we tend to lead with emotions—it is one of our better qualities. As leaders we tend to be transformational as we emotionally invest ourselves in our team. At home we do the same; thus, when someone around us is emotionally off kilter, we feel we need to fix it, make them all better. This is taking their "junk" and making it ours, making it personal. Ask yourself, "Is it possible this has nothing to do with me?"

Reminder: I suggest you take an actual Q-TIP and tape it to an index card, your portfolio, next to your phone, wherever you find your triggers are hit. It's a nice, private reminder to Quit Taking It Personally.

Create a "what if" plan.

This is a readiness plan. What if you lose your job tomorrow? Have a large expenditure? Loss of computer files? Kids have a snow day? Do you know where everything you need is, if you need it in a jiff? Do you have a backup sitter plan? Friends you can lean on and share with?

Be sure to share this with your loved ones or, if the plan is work-related, a colleague. I even keep an emergency stash of stress relief (chocolate, bath salts, bottle of wine, and candles).

The irony is having this stash is like having a safety net. I know I have it in times of emergency. In being prepared for the "what ifs," you mentally relax, making you more resilient.

Being resilient also equates to asking for help when it is needed. Did you know men are just as willing to lift the dishes out of the dishwasher if they are asked...and then are appreciated for doing so? What I mean by this is if you ask for help, and you should, be sure you remember they are going to do it their way and you need to appreciate that. Hey, it's one reason we married them. The opposite is also true: if you ask and then berate the job they did, you won't get the help next time you ask. According to Wattis, Standing, and Yerkes, (2013) men respond to positive reinforcement just as much as women do. However, neither gender is a mind reader—so right back to communication.

Lauran Star

Eat More Cake

I am a baker, not a cake eater...

At work we set meetings or appointments up to get stuff done, but in the home we want "spontaneous." We all have heard the "experts in balance" talk about setting up date nights or sex nights, but what is missing in this equation is energy. Life takes a ton of energy and it is give and take. It is great to set up a date with your partner or spouse, but if you are lacking the overall energy, what good is the time spent together? The first thing we need to look at is where you are spending your time and energy.

Stop looking at all the things you need to do on your planner or phone and instead see it as pie or cake. Mine is dark chocolate with fudge frosting. Each slice of cake is energy, and I get to select whom my cake goes to.

Energy: Think of energy level as slices of cake. Every day we wake up with a full chocolate fudge cake to hand out or eat. It is full when we awake and then during the day we unconsciously eat or give away slices. Some people take more cake (cake eaters) and others give us cake (bakers). *However, until you start thinking about cake as energy you give away, you* *will never know how much you have or who is stealing that gooey slice from you.*

Your goal is to give and take slices during the work day so you can return home with half a cake or more; thus, you will have energy for your home life. Some days you will have more cake than others, as the daily interactions of cake eaters and bakers changes.

Cake eaters are those to whom you give a slice or two during the day, and yes some cake eaters will even go as far as to steal a slice. These are events or people that you expend energy on without full awareness. Cake eaters are not always easy to spot, such as a friend or co-worker who always burdens you with their problems in hopes you will have a solution.

However you have the choice whether to give a slice or to keep it. A meeting where you have to be "on" is also giving a few slices away. Both at work and home, tasks are cake eating. **Bakers**, however, are the opposite. They give you a slice of their cake, and sometimes it is even a better flavor of the cake you woke up with. These are friends or colleagues who give you energy. Bakers can be events or tasks that give you goose bumps. One of my bakers is youth coaching—I just love empowering your girls on the lacrosse field—it gives me energy!

Examples:

Cake Eaters	Bakers
• Stress	• Working out
• Meetings	• Reading a good book
• Friends who whine	• Laughter
• Poor eating habits	• A good friend
• Poor relationships	• Coaching
• External Family Members	• Sex
	• Family Members

The majority of the time, we are unaware where our cake goes during the day, only to find we are cake-less when we return home. This is where stress raises its ugly head and emotional and resiliency goes right out the door. Cake awareness is a tool you can use anywhere, as often I will make the comment "nope, not sharing my cake today" as a means to give myself permission to take a "me" day.

So let's look at your cake...

Think about today and where your cake was eaten. Who got slices and who gave slices? Mark your cake so you can see where it went. Note how much cake you had left at 3:00 p.m. and then at 6:00 p.m. Who did you give cake to, were you surprised who got cake without asking for it? Can you see where cake is gained? It is amazing once we start to see where our energy is going how we can quickly take control and keep what we need. What is also amazing is where your cake goes during the day; understanding where it goes also helps build personal self- awareness.

Let's face it, at the end of the day we all wish we had more energy. The keeper, however, is you are in charge of your energy output. It really does come down to you. The slices are given by you; thus, if you want more cake you need to decide to keep some. Once you take accountability for the lack of energy, you will quickly find ways to improve.

SHIFTING PARADIGMS

So here is your cake. Photocopy several cakes, one for each day, and over the next week write down everywhere you give a slice and who takes a slice. Go ahead and have fun with this— use colored markers or pens.

After you have done five to seven days of cake, ask yourself:

- Where is cake gained and lost?
- Who is taking your cake that surprised you?
- How much cake are you saving for your family? For you?
- Where will you change who gets a slice?
- What will you now do with the extra slices you have?

Are you surprised? This is a great exercise to do if you find at the end of the day you are without any energy. Have your family do this exercise. When my kids complain that they do not have time for homework, I give them a copy of the cake and have them take a few minutes to see where they wasted time and energy. Even my ten-year-olds get it, and make comments around who ate their cake that day.

When you identify your cake eaters, you have a choice: do you keep the slice or continue to give it away? In the end, it really is up to you.

BEING PRESENT TO ENJOY YOUR CAKE_____

This is one of the harder strategies we as humans need to work on. We have become a culture of multitasking, being multi-minded and multi-focused. As technology advances the line between work and home becomes more and more blurred.

When we are at home, our minds are busy with work, and at work, busy with home. I have clients who journal while they sleep—in fits of wakefulness they grab pen and paper to clear their mind.

We teach our children to supersize, do more, be more, multitask, and spread themselves so thin that success is out of reach. Then we are at a loss when the child's mood/attitude sours. They too struggle with being present.

My daughter, elementary school age, made a comment one day when we examined her spelling test..."Mom it was so hard today taking this test—the room was noisy, my tummy was hungry, and all I could think about was being a veterinarian (we just got a new puppy) and a rock star." So I asked her how she overcame..."I wrote a rock song about Loki (our puppy) while taking the test."

The kicker: when we focus elsewhere, we are telling whoever is around us they do not matter as much as whatever we are thinking. Multi-focus is done both unconsciously and consciously and is contagious. If our minds drift, others follow. This equally affects work and home, but the damage can be seen differently as at work the job itself may suffer, and at home your loved ones and emotions may suffer.

Mindfulness is quickly becoming a cash cow as there are well over 8,000 titles on Amazon about mindfulness (Cole, 2014). Yet what does mindfulness really mean? Simply put, it is being in the moment, and yes, it falls under Emotional Intelligence and thus it is learnable. It is the inner calm that brings you back to center, regardless of the situation. The kicker: you already know how to reach present, so stop spending money on techniques and start apply them, as there is no magic pill or path to being present with those you care about.

So how can we be present?
Self-awareness

This little skill packs a huge punch as it is the first step in being present, thus, you guessed it: Journal! Identify what situations or triggers shift your focus, when are you not present, when did you need to be, where did you go. Once this is noted, you can calmly define how you would like to react to this trigger. Writing down your reaction and thoughts helps to build neuro-pathways in the brain, helping you remember next time.

Pay attention to your environment

Listen to what is being said, and monitor body language. Look for the external clues that will give you internal perception as to where both you and a peer truly are emotionally. Don't be afraid to openly, one on one, identify what you think you are hearing or seeing. Validation is a powerful tool! It is not enough to be empathetic; you must share that with the person for whom you are feeling empathy.

Get on their level

Regardless of whom you're speaking with, be sure you're eye to eye.

When I am chatting with my children, I drop to one knee so that we are eye level. This places me "in the moment" as the physical movement triggers my focus on them. I do the same with my husband: as he is a note taker, I grab a pad of paper when we talk and then take notes. It is the physical reminder that I am present.

Stress is the number one trigger to not being present

We are faced with stress both at home and work, but how you react can be a critical sign you are no longer engaged in the interaction. Become aware of how YOU react to stress. Is it physical? For example, your shoulders tighten, your jaw clenches, and you get a headache or your heart rate increases. Is it emotional, presented as yelling, crying, screaming, or withdrawal? When you feel stressed, do a body check. Stress causes body issues you may not even be aware of, and therefore your body is like a stress beacon for you.

Breathe

Believe it or not, just breathing can bring you right back to the moment. Find your quiet place. This can be anywhere, as long as you are comfortable.

- SLOWLY breathe in through your nose, expanding your abdominal muscles while inhaling.
- Now hold your breath for three seconds...one one-thousand...two one-thousand...three one-thousand.
- Slowly exhale out your mouth. This need not be a quiet exhale; it may be beneficial to hear the air leave your body, thus clearing your mind and body of any negativity and stress.
- REPEAT. Deep breathe three or four times.

Sounds easy right? Breathe when you are stressed, just before a meeting, when you are having a conversation with a family member, or anytime you need to be PRESENT.

People you work with and/or you love do not know you care until you are present.

Chapter 6

Success is Not a Solo Task

If success were solo, who would celebrate your wins and help you up when you fall?

Success Does Not Have to Be Lonely

There is no "I" in success, so stop going it alone.
Create your own unique success team and the world is yours.

I often wonder, why do women feel they need to go it alone when striving for success? Why do some thrive in success while others hide? What are we afraid of? Why do we not reach out to others when we need help? Is it fear of failure or fear of success? The kicker is, there is no "I" in success; reaching success alone is almost impossible, so stop going it by yourself.

What are you afraid of?

Before you can achieve or begin to build your success team, you need to uncover what is holding you back. The fear of success and the fear of failure are two entire worlds apart, and the end results are different. I recently asked a group of 500 women what they were more afraid of, success or failure. Ninety-eight percent noted they were afraid of failure, but in truth what they were scared of was in fact success. See, we fail all the time. We know how to cope with failure. In risk taking and failing comes a learning process—and sometimes the best ideas. Women are not afraid to fail, they are afraid to succeed—they just do not know it.

189

What is success?

Success is for some an unknown. Often they cannot tell you how to reach it let alone what it looks like once they get there. There is no clear and defined path for success. Once success is reached we look around and then wonder … now what or what do I do with this success. How do I respond to being successful? No wonder we are afraid of success. Even I suffer from this fear of success from time to time. When we enter the workforce, no one gives us a book or tool that outlines what success is. The reason: defining success is different for everyone. When we have a fear of success, we often find ourselves procrastinating (it took me two years to write this book) or self-sabotaging (allowing other stuff to get in the way). Guilt can come into play if you feel you do not deserve success. Negative self-talk can also be an obstacle that should be shut that down quickly. When negative talk enters my mind, I immediately ask, "Says who?" Women tend to overindulge in negative self –talk and we need to shift and move on. Once you pivot and say to yourself- and believe it, "No more—I deserve success and am not afraid of it," you can then move forward.

The first step in overcoming the fear of success is to take the emotions out of success. Fear is just an emotion and we need to neutralize it to move around it. Typically once we kick fear out of the equation, the pathway to success becomes clear.

So how do we end the reign of terror? As successful as I have been, honestly I still fear it. However now I no longer allow the fear to rule my actions. I take the emotions out of it and below is how.

Asked yourself:

What does success look like to me? How do I define success?

It is not surprising that you may have to really ponder these questions. We enter the world of leadership, motherhood, entrepreneurship and life and often forget to ask what success is. This may take you a bit to truly answer for yourself.

I spent years struggling with this question, *Am I successful?* Even while knee deep in corporate America climbing the ladder to "success." I was financially accomplished, yet I was not fulfilled. The money just bought things. At the end of the day, I would close the books, head home, and look for gratification there. I would spend time with my husband and close friends. Still, in the morning I would don my office face and off to work I would go again. I had no idea what I needed (no, wanted) for success—what it looked like, how to reach it and its purpose. I felt many times I was a fake, not truly being me. Sure, I could get the job done and then some and was rewarded with promotions and money, but I was still empty. Until I defined what success was to me, I was walking around in a fog. The sad part is, I defined success for myself in my early 40s. That's a long work history of walking around unfulfilled and unsure if I was successful.

Success to me is the ability to make an impact on both my generation and the next with a focus on women's empowerment. Clearly stated, I am successful when I can help another person get ahead or achieve their goals. In one sense, this is what made me an accomplished leader in the corporate world, but that was only a token of my world. In the end, it is not how much money I make. I give because I can and it fills me. The money follows the passion, not the other way around.

The kicker- success looks different for every hat you wear. As a mom of three my success equation looks very different than that of work.

Once I focused on what success meant to me, the path to my success became clear. You see, rather than being lodged in the problem of women struggling to advance, I became a solution. I had to take myself out of the corporate equation and add myself to my passion and success result. Let me show you how easy it can be... if this is what you really want.

What gifts do I already have in place to achieve? I like to call this taking stock in what you have and what you need to flourish. Are you a selfless giver, a nurturer, teacher? How do you communicate with others—do you "just" connect with people? What skills do you have? We dove deeper on this topic in "What is your Superpower" (Chapter 3). Make a true list or get creative and make a photo poster of all the superpowers you have. Keep it close by so when fear shows it head you can remind yourself that you really ROCK!

Is it the same as the person next to you? How is success different for your partner or spouse? Does it matter to you what another's success looks like? I actively ask this question to all my friends and colleagues, at business conferences and roundtables. While their success may not have an impact on yours, you may have something to offer to help them move forward. In sharing how you define success, you in turn invite another to help you and you them. It also helps kick fear in the rear.

What are my gains if I am successful? This is my favorite question as it is the WIFM: *"What Is In It For Me"* if I am successful. What would life be like? Can you picture it? A vision board works well here. I am a colorful person, so when I define what my wins will look like I use colored markers. Green for money...and then what I want that money to buy, Pink for my two daughters, blue for my son; I keep in mind my triumphs will affect my children one way or another. Red is for my relationship with my husband, and coral is for just me. What will I gain from this?

What is the downfall of being successful? Here is where we begin to truly neutralize fear. What is the worst thing that will happen if I am successful? We need to uncover what the risk is to being successful. Are you afraid you will become a different person? Will people ask you for money (that is one of my issues)? Where does guilt come in? Remember we all know how to fail, so that cannot be one of your answers here. Are you afraid the higher you climb the further you can fall? Remember, touching the clouds of amazement is a lifetime chance. You can only fall if you see the fall as detrimental to yourself, instead of a new challenge. Keep in mind, success is NOT linear; it is ups and downs, rights and lefts along the path.

How will others react to your success? This was a fear for me, as I learned from past examples other people would dump their junk on me. I would listen and take it as my own, adding my baggage to deal with. Comments like "wow this was so easy for you...not like you had to work for it... and a more recent one -do they just hire anyone..." is their junk, not yours. I have had to learn to stop listening, to tune out. I know who will celebrate with me and who will attempt to make me feel unjustified. Guess what, I no longer share my victories with those who are not on my train! I choose who hears and who does not, who I share my wine with and who can #@*!#!

How am I stopping myself from reaching my stars?
Notice, I say you are stopping yourself. How are you blocking your own path? It could be by focusing your efforts elsewhere and getting caught up in the minutiae of business. You allow yourself to think small picture versus end goals. You use the words, "I can't" or "I do not know how." Compose a list and determine how you will resolve this. Keep this list handy as you may be adding to it.

Ask yourself why you deserve the success—or do you?
Self-doubt is the dark angel of fear. All it takes is a dash of uncertainty and you are off track and in the weeds. We all deserve respect and rewards.

How do I get there? It is important to have a plan for success. That being said, keep in mind a good plan is flexible. It needs to allow for life to intervene and play. A good plan is just a road map – not the road. You want to be sure, while your plan is in play, you do not miss out on the good stuff so keep your eyes open on your journey.

Pivotal Woman

Lisa Schermerhorn CH, RMT is a leading expert on success—she has worked with hundreds of women helping them get over the fear of success,

Why are women afraid of success? What do you see in your practice? There are many reasons that women can be afraid of success and much of it has to do with the way they are "programmed" as children. A child's brain frequency is much different than that of an adult. What children experience between birth and nineteen becomes their "**normal**." When we are young we learn what love is, the significance of money, how to relationship, you develop your work ethic and what safety and security looks like.

Religion, culture, and trauma can also have a large impact on the way we behave as adults. There are many cultures and religions that will not permit a woman to be successful and/or independent. In order to break with those norms, sometimes women may be forced to leave their family or break from their religious beliefs. This is their support system and for most people, just the thought of that can be reason enough to be afraid of success.

Understand why you have this fear, then deal with it and move on. Uncover where the fear stems from and you are a step closer to destroying the fear. Begin to develop a dynasty of individuals who can act as a mirror and show you your true self.

One of the most effective ways of moving forward is to have a success team, Your Success Team. We cannot know it all or do it all. Successful men and women have one thing in common: they have a group of individuals/colleagues and friends backing them. In the next section we will be taking a deeper look into creating your own success team focused on your growth.

Building Your Success Team

I like to think of success as playing the game of Survivor®, *where it boils down to alliances getting you ahead.*

In life, that is exactly how you get ahead. It is more about who you know than what you know. There have been numerous articles written on the need for women to have an advisory board/success team in place. The attention it receives is due to the fact that it works; men have this success team in place. In a prolific success team, gender does not matter; in fact, for women, I highly encourage you to have at least two men you can go to with questions or guidance. Why? They often have a deeper awareness of how the organization works—who does what and who gets it done. If your success plan is focused in growth within a structured workplace, Organizational Awareness is critical. If your success is outside these constructs, then it may not be critical; however, if you are working in any manner with companies you must understand who the buyers are, what their needs are, who has the cash flow, who are the decision makers, when does conflict arise (because it will) how do they manage it.

There is nothing like a concrete life plan to weigh you down. Because if you always have one eye on some future goal, you stop paying attention to the job at hand, miss opportunities that might arise, and stay fixedly on one path, even when a better, newer course might have opened up.
Indra Nooyi,
CEO of PepsiCo

To build a strong team we first must start with your dynasty. This is the first brick in your team and often you may find you can stop here if you do not work for an organization. Those of us who are entrepreneurs tend to lead with dynasty and success follows. If you are working within a structured confines of a company or organization you will need to continue to lead with organizational awareness and then build your success team.

YOUR DYNASTY

Women tend to go it alone...sound familiar? Men, however, create a clan/tribe. Men network differently than women; they are connected and understand the power dynamics and influence paradigms in the workforce by having strong associations in place.

I empower you to build your dynasty of connections into an empire. Let me clarify a few things. There is a huge difference between tribe and dynasty members. Dynasty members are your go-to people regardless of gender.

There has been much work on tribe and clan mentality. What I am pivoting to is more dynasty or your legacy of connections. A tribe is your group of followers who tweet about you and your stuff. They are the connections on LinkedIn, Facebook, Twitter, Google+, YouTube and all other social media accounts. The connection to tribe members is usually via only social media, and they too are critical in driving your message and brand, so show them the love!

A dynasty has more touch points. Members share information, and we tend to stay connected via e-mail and phone calls. There is a closeness and trust instinct with dynasty members as they are rooting for your success. Dynasty members have more skin in the game and the benefits are HUGE.

Who is in your dynasty?
Do you have a go-to list of individuals you can call on for information, coverage, mirror holders and so forth? There are individuals that are in your corner, that have your back. Some you may have met while others are connected via the World Wide Web. How far is your reach? See, the caveat of having a dynasty is that it takes work, more work than building a tribe. It is a true give-and-take relationship. It is creating a list of

what their strengths are and how you can help them. These are close connections, not Facebook pals.

The Lauran Dynasty

I have strong, independent, soft, wise, young and caring men and women in my dynasty. I have a few stay-at-home moms who adore my kids and are there for them if need be. I have authors, coaches, moms, dads, and thought leaders, and I look for a dash of diversity. My dynasty is gender- and generation-neutral as diversity rocks!

It is simple to create a lasting dynasty. First, focus on what your career is, and who else plays there. What do you need in your career, and who can help you achieve it? Next, look at thought leadership—who shares the same ideas as you? What topics do you want more information on? Then family life—to whom are you connected at home? Joiners of all groups are there to help you get ahead and you them. It is a co-creative relationship.

Once you identify who, then take action. Follow who you need to follow, and participate in their discussions. It is NOT enough to just link or follow them—you have to engage, comment, and retweet. You need to create a connection, not begin stalking. Get involved in their thought leadership. Share ideas, or, if you find something interesting, bring it to their attention.

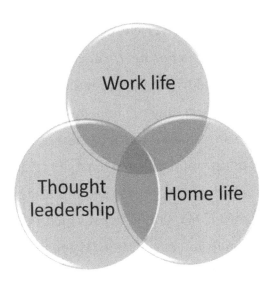

If you want me to belong to your dynasty, I have to feel a connection. Once the connection is made and I see the investment you share with me, I am honored to be part of your dynasty. If you need something, shoot me an e-mail—do not ping me, as you are dynasty. You have earned the right once the true connection is made.

You can add circles to you dynasty as you move forward. I have nine circles (home, work, speaking, thought leadership, author, publicity, legal, and consulting). The amazing part of creating circles in your dynasty is when I can share the connections with others in my dynasty. The dynasty sweet spot! When writing this book, and I needed more information or thought leadership, I reached out to those I have a connection with first.

Forewarning, I try to keep my dynasty manageable. My focus is on ten people in each circle, otherwise I am spread too thin. My dynasty is an area I protect. They are the closest links I have in social media and friendship. I send them all personalize holiday cards, know when they are in need of help, speak with them on the phone and am part of their success plan as they are part of mine. In my opinion, my dynasty is all about **quality NOT quantity**, and while others may see this as a hole in my empire, the key word is MY. I only invest time in those who invest in me, and I give you permission (if you need it) to do the same.

I have many followers and am blessed for them. On my Pivot blog, thought leaders in my circles share and give a deluge of information and insights to my readers. These are tweeted and shared throughout social media. These are my tribe members and are to be treasured with gifts of awareness and insight. I treat them with love and respect and am attentive to their needs. Your tribe versus your dynasty is a shift in focus to be all about them and what they need to succeed. I love all of Seth Godin's work on tribes. His work on how tribes help us all change our future is amazing.

In understanding the gender differences and seeing them through a new lens, you open yourself up to endless opportunities to flourish and attract those who will benefit you the most. Or you can keep on looking at gender as "us versus them"...the choice is yours and the results are too.

We all need a dynasty due to life changing. If you have a strong dynasty and you lose your job you have the connections already in place to gain new employment. Think of the last downsize in your company. Did some appear to get lucky and find employment within a few days or weeks? That is not luck my dear – that was her dynasty.

From your dynasty now begin to create Your Success Team

Focus on Organizational Awareness_____

This is the understanding of how leadership, as well as how the organization, functions and performs, along with its abilities, potential, and results. It is a clear understanding of how the subgroups or departments function under the organizational umbrella. It is a look into how conflict, purchasing decisions, change, and needs are managed. It is an understanding of who the players are, what political forces are present, and how the outside world interacts with the internal facets of business.

One way to gain a better feel for organizational awareness is to dissect an opportunity you were aware of and answer the following questions below. Write all the answers down and see if you can find a pattern. I love doing this and find that the information gained is valuable. Think of it like a board game. Your answers do not have to be formal or pretty, they need to be factual.

- Who were the players?
- What fence were they on in respect to the issue?
- Who won or got the results they were looking for?
- How did they do that?
- Whom did they work with?
- Was it ethical?
- Did the results benefit a department or the entire system?

To confess, every time I start a new contract, I play this game. I have fun pulling the organization apart to find areas of weakness and strengths, allies and power struggles. I wish I only had this knowledge twenty years ago; I would have definitely climbed higher and had a lot more fun while stepping up.

Now, take these answers and apply them to your success
goals.

- Who are the players for your success?
- Where do they fall: pro or con?
- Who do they know to help you move forward?
- If you do not know them directly, who does?
- What do you bring to their table?
- How will helping you benefit them?

As women, our business shortcomings fall to the lack of
comfort in asking for help when we need it, networking, and
keeping our personal power. Notice I said we lack comfort,
meaning all we need to do is increase our exposures, add a few
tools and bingo. Once you uncover what success looks like to
you, now ask who can help you achieve it and what do you
need. Compile a list of things and people you need in your
corner.

SHIFTING PARADIGMS

Who do you go to lunch with, or what people do you know
that can get you ahead where you're working? More often than
not, we choose to go socialize during lunch with our buddies,
but those who are movers and shakers know whom to eat with.
We are human beings, thus we seek comfort over discomfort.
That being said, to get ahead you need to stop wasting time
living in comfort and start looking for opportunities.

BUILDING YOUR SUCCESS TEAM (YST)_____

YST is a tribe of your people whom you trust, much like your dynasty however are focused within one organization and will help you see your blind spots, hold a mirror up and show you the truth. They have insider insight and may have been where you are heading or where you are right now. They are men and women, multi-generational, a variety of ranks and levels within a corporation. While I like the number of five (5) for my team, their reach is ten-fold. A fruitful team receives as much as it gives, as it is a two way street and it takes time to build.

Trust is like a red wine glass. Once it is broken, no amount of glue will put it back together. There will always be leakage of precious wine.

From an Organizational Standpoint:

- Identify who you would like in your corner.
- What skills/influences do they possess that you need? What do you have that they may need?
- How are they seen in the company? Will that help or hurt you?
- Do you have a relationship with these people? If not, who does? What connections do you need to make a connection?

- How do you build a relationship with them? This is usually the one area women truly struggle with. I focus on this a bit more in Chapter 9, but you cannot just walk up to someone, male or female, and ask them to be in your corner. There needs to be a relationship there based on honest interest. Get to know the person first, what you share in common, what projects they are working on, and where you can help them. Often offering help is a trusted way to build a relationship.

Be open and honest with those in your corner. Be transparent in what your needs and desires are and share them with your team. Uncover what they need and help them achieve it. Motivate each other. Be open and honest with each other—trust is the YST building block.

I always did something I was a little not ready to do. I think that's how you grow. When there's that moment of 'Wow, I'm not really sure I can do this,' and you push through those moments, that's when you have a breakthrough.
Marissa Mayer, CEO of Yahoo!

Okay, I have an YST. Now what?

Get the team together monthly or quarterly and mastermind. Think outside the box about how you can help each other and pivot. Identify where you are each struggling and help identify blind spots and networking opportunities.

Re-evaluate your goals for the YST every six months so that you do not miss anything along the way. Share and celebrate everyone's success!

The Sandbox
Where to Find Other Great Women

I found my best friends and allies in sandboxes; all I had to do was dig in and share my toys.

Ever notice kids at a playground are very selective with whom they share their toys with? They are just as selective with whom they allow in their sandbox, and more importantly, which sandboxes to play in. They are very careful to play with other children who can either get them the toy they want, children they can lead, or children who share the same sand theme. The amazing part of children in sandboxes: they come in all colors, genders and sizes and never take it personally when the sandbox does not meet their playing needs. They just move to another sandbox.

As adults, we too play in sandboxes. Examples are where you work, the organization you work with, where you let your hair down and with whom and of course where you network. That being said, the largest difference today versus when we were children is biased selectivity. By a show of hands, how many of you belong to women-only sandboxes. And now, let us ask the bigger question: are they helping you or hurting you?

Some all-female groups are beneficial depending on what your needs are or why you are there, but studies demonstrate more and more selective biased networking groups do not work if you are looking for career advancement. Why? The focus or perspective they bring to the table is one-sided and lacks inclusion of diversity.

Research has shown women are falling short in the *right* sandbox finding, and it is no wonder. First, it is not a comfort zone for us; imagine being in a room of 100 women and being asked to share what you need...umm, hello vulnerability, never mind adding our issues of success failure and the need to appear confident and knowledgeable. It is not surprising the answer we tend to hear when that question is raised is how we overcome our own needs or how we are so successful. Nope, not going to share, going to take my sand toys home and hide them because I do not want to be judged or stolen from.

Adding fuel to the fire, women tend to network with women-only groups, and my personal favorite is moms' groups. Let's get a group of moms together and compare child rearing notes—HA. Women tend to be one of the most unfriendly, competitive groups of people on earth. No, ladies I am not saying we are bad people, but it is just the social dynamic and corresponding actions when you place a group of women together.

Think back to high school, if you need a reminder. What

social group did you belong to, and where was your rank in that group? This competition starts at a very young age and is reinforced by our culture. *You are not thin enough, you should marry up, if you purchase the right stuff and hang with the "in" crowd you will have arrived.* This is all, quite simply put, bullshit. In any group of individuals, it can quickly become the "one-up man or woman show." We see this more so in gender-neutral groups and it is also very biased.

Case in point: when I hung my consulting shingle out, I immediately joined several women-only groups. Hey, they are my clients so why not? What I found was, I ended up out of money. I was spending a few thousands of dollars on groups that honestly after the first few meetings revealed they did not meet my needs. Trust me, I am no wallflower, so before any of you say "you get what you put into the group," there are bigger questions to ask. I am a doer, meaning if I see an issue, I dive right in to fix it. I'm the go-to gal. I have sat as board member, program director, learning and training vice president, and more—only to find not only was it sucking the time out of my schedule, but it also could become all-consuming if I let it.

I reached out to a past colleague who was once my manager, and he asked me to re-think how I saw networking. He, a man who was very high up on the corporate ladder, noted he never spent a dime on network groups or professional associations unless the return on investment was present and obvious at the purchase point. Networking groups are a business where you are paying someone to bring you all together, so be sure you fit before you buy. He reminded me I would not purchase a sweater without trying it on, sometime several different times. The greatest suggestion was to ask first what I can do to improve this group—is it worth my time or is there a greater return on investment? If not, then get out of dodge.

Networking is part of life—we all know to get ahead, it is who you know. There is a fee for this knowledge, and while my past mentor rose in a climate where networking groups were not as fruitful, it is savvy to know where you are spending your time and money.

SHIFTING PARADIGMS_____

Look at all the networking groups that are businesses and then the ones you belong to and ask yourself, what is the *return on investment for YOU* in this group? Even if the group is free, what are you getting from it? What critical connections did you make? How much does the membership, plus meetings, travel and time cost you? To figure this out, I add an hourly rate in: how much money did I lose by being at the meeting versus working on my own stuff? What did you gain in the meeting?

Was it a bunch of business cards yet when you get home you have no idea who gave you what? What are you giving them? Are you a member of the board (for free)? Are you mentoring others in the group? Does the association true have your needs at heart or are they a contradiction?

I do this once a year with all my associations and networks. It keeps me honest with my time because in the end, that is the one thing I truly need more of.

Take a look at where you're playing right now, or wish to play, and ask yourself:

Do you have networking goals for this group? What do want to give and receive from this group? What is the goal of the group? Do they achieve that goal? How are they connected?

I am not the only one noting the disparity in networking for women, as *Forbes* writer Meghan Casserly and other pivotal women look at this topic based on Athena Vongalis-Macrow's work in this area. In her article she disclosed four important questions surrounding women networking groups.

1. *Who is in the network?* Who are the players, and are they at the same level you are or above you? You are only as valuable at your top five network connections in wealth. If you take the sum of each of the five's income

and divide by five that is the money ceiling of worth for the network.

2. ***How well does the network connect?*** Is the network an exclusion to themselves only or are they nationwide? Do they allow experts to come in or keep it to just to membership? This is where we see a large bias in perspectives as the network becomes the only voice or right way to achieve success.

3. ***How do they share or communicate?*** In today's social media world, networks communicate, at times, extensively. What I am exploring here is what are they communicating—are they transparent in their vision or is it the board's decision? When a member makes noise, do they listen or give them the company line (I am the noise maker so I hear the line all the time—then take my toys and go home, their loss). Are they reinvesting in the network's goals or keeping the money for themselves?

4. ***Who are you talking to?*** So when you go to audition a network, who is approachable? Who are you spending your time with, like-minded, same-level individuals or are you pushing the envelope? I would push it, as it is a wonderful way to examine access within the group and discover the power struggles.

Now I am not saying never join a networking group; what I am suggesting is to join the right networking group and be skillful regardless if it is a networking group or association. I also encourage you to balance your female-only groups with a few co-gendered groups. Hey, I love my women's groups. They bring me outstanding connections, inspiration, perspective, a leg up at times, and a ton of laughs. Be that as it may, I have a clear understanding of what I need to get and give from these groups.

I never go to professional programs that cost less than I make in a day. Personal and business development, thought leadership beyond your level, and content-driven solutions cost money.

It is not unheard of for a women's group to be focused on just super cool chicks, like *Women Inspiring Women in New Hampshire*, where the focus is on women networking and sharing peer-to-peer fun and education. This group is truly filled with *super fun and cool chicks*, and the CEO, Leslie Sturgeon, gives more than she gets—this group gives her goose bumps. Knowing this is the goal of the group when I attend, I am there to laugh, connect, share myself and embrace just being female.

Another group I belong to is *Ellevate*, led by Sallie Krawcheck. While this group is all powerful executive women, the end focus is women connecting with women all over the country at a variety of levels. It is about ensuring you invest in yourself as well as a plethora of business information. They have member spotlights, newsletters, teleconferences, meetings, and are nationwide. Here the return on investment is easy to find as the connections made will help you move forward in your career.

How do you approach meetings and events? Is the meeting over an hour away? Will you be routinely going? Can you schedule the first three meetings in your daytimes or by phone? What is your plan for the group—will you be sitting on the side line or jumping in?

What are you receiving from the group? That is correct: what do you need to get from this group to make your time worth attendance? If you do not know, do not go. I suggest setting up two or three goals for each group you network with for every meeting you go to—and every time. It may be as simple as resolving to make three solid connections tonight (not just grabbing their business cards). Or it could be as complex as resolving to uncover the training needs for company X by meeting with Susan.

What do they need from you? All successful networks require a give and take. If one party is doing all the giving, the network relationship is not balanced. You have to give to get; with that said, however, wait until you are with a group for at least six months before stepping up. It takes about six to eight months to determine if this group is for you. If they ask you to help out prior to your own knowledge that this group is for you, then pass. Let them know you are still feeling the group out.

Is there a hierarchy in the group, and do you fit it? Do you like the people in the group? Are they your people? Do they get you? How safe do you feel in the group? Do you have a role or know where will you fit in the hierarchy? Most importantly, will you step out of your safety bubble and explore, or will you just float in the group? Safety is a relative term, as we all need physical and emotional safety. However, in networking we also need to feel secure enough to be authentic to ourselves. This may come over time, so if you're uncomfortable today, try again. If after six months you're still on edge, leave.

Ask for a reference. Send an e-mail asking to speak to a few members who go regularly to see if this group is for you. I will even go as far as to select whom I want to chat with, by trialing the membership space—selecting five members and sending them e-mails asking what they like and do not like about the group. Networking is a business, and they have to earn the right to your business. This will also give you a few connections before the first meeting so you are not going in blind.

Are you authentic to yourself, or are you authentic to the group? Who shows up when you go to the meeting? There have been many a meeting where I would leave and then ask myself who the hell was I just then? We all put on the happy perfect façade when meeting new people. This takes a ton of energy, especially if you have to do this for the whole meeting. Strong connections are made when you are just you—the real you. I am direct, hate being sold to and will not compete at a networking gig. In fact, if you try this with me I usually will psychoanalyze you the Lauran Star way—fun for me, not you. Hey, it is who I am. I want to know the real you, and if you are not willing to show it after we have met several times, I am done playing with your toys.

When people ask what you do, tell them what your passion is. It is easy to get caught up in the *what do you do game*, so instead of sharing your career, share your passion. This changes the dynamic of the conversation and will give you a true sense of the membership. When asked what I do, I could create a laundry list of things that in the end would feel like I am selling myself to you. Instead, I share my passion of wine or female empowerment. I neutralize the emotion of competition or at least try to, as some would still out-man me here.

Is there a balance? *The balance question is the critical one. Balance = ROI.* Is there enough balance in the group to provide you with what you need? Is there a bigger perspective you can gain knowledge from? In diversity comes balance as it opens doors that otherwise are closed. Do you belong to a group where you all make the same amount of money in the same field at the same level? If you answered yes, I hope the goal for you here is just fun, not advancement. Balance comes from fields, salary, gender, career levels, and so much more. There are groups in every industry that are focused on that specific field, but is there diversity in the career levels, perspectives, and other backgrounds of those in membership?

You can apply all these questions to any network group, be it in person, Facebook with page likes, LinkedIn with groups or other professional organizations. With social media one needs to be careful when joining groups. Be sure you are not spreading yourself too thin, as it is easy to join a group and then not play there. Every December 29th I look at all my LinkedIn groups and Facebook pages and decided where I stay and where I go. My personal brand is about empowerment and engagement, so if I am in a group that I do not play in, my own brand comes into question (for me anyways). Never mind the benefit of decreased e-mails from these groups.

So how do we find these amazing networking sandboxes?

There is no magic trick here. Look at your professional associations and ask those you look up to where they network. If you have a LinkedIn profile, where are you connected, what groups do you participate in, where do your links play? All you need do is look up their profile. At work, listen to where senior leadership "hangs out." Great groups do not just appear—you have to look for them. Use the connections you have today to further relate tomorrow.

THE GREAT MENTOR DEBATE_____

If you have been living outside the shelter of a rock you have heard women need mentors. There is a deluge of research on this topic, and why not—it is how men ascended the ranks in the past. I am all for mentors, I have had several and, a little secret, they were mostly men. I know, curse me—however, when I was mounting the business world, those ahead of me were men, so I utilized their insight. Men are not afraid of sharing the "how to "for their advancement. They do not feel they need to hold it close to the vest for fear you will steal their secrets. They approach mentoring with the "I will show you the how, yet you need to still do the work" mentality.

What studies also show us is that women tend to go ahead alone (Ragins & Cotton, 2014). For a variety of reasons, women with mentors climb faster and are happier. Organizations seeing the value in mentorship currently have initiatives in place in hopes to decrease the number of barriers and increase women in senior leadership positions with mentors. Studies also show those who have a mentor tend to make more money, have a higher level of job satisfaction, are more willing to mentor the next in line, and overall have improved life satisfaction.

Women with mentors are no longer alone in the business world, and the number one reason why women tend not to have a mentor is the fear of asking for one (Roche, n.d.).

So what is mentoring?

It is an ongoing process of sharing ideas and shortening the learning curve for the mentee. It does not happen overnight. It is not just given away, as it is something that takes hard work on both sides. Mentoring is not limited to the workplace, as there are multiple rewards for mentoring the youth.

FINDING YOUR MENTOR_____

Stop putting it off. Find your mentor today; while it may
take time to find the right one for you, you need to start
looking today.

Identify what skills you need to add to your tool box.
Look at past performance reviews to determine where you
need to develop. Ask your supervisor if you can take a 360
assessment (usually Human Resources will have this), or
contact me and I can get it set up for you. This type of
assessment asks your peers where you need to work and
where your strengths lie. Assimilate a list of five areas and then
begin to look at who you know and see who has those skills.

Uncover those you know who could mentor you. Then
begin the task of asking. Ask men and women whom you look
up to and have a relationship with to mentor you—do not be
shy...ask for what you want. Surprisingly, if they know you the
answer will be yes. If you find someone whom you do not
know, begin to create a relationship with them before asking.
In other words, before you ask me, know me. Mentoring is
work, and the relationship is critical. We both need to be on the
same page—have a co-creative link. I may be the best mentor
in the world, but if we clash on a personality level, I will do you
no good.

Just because she is a woman does not mean she is the best mentor or that she should mentor you. She may not have time to mentor you, or the connection is just not there. You may gain more insight from a male mentor, depending on where you need to focus. To be honest, I personally am tired of hearing all the mantra on how women need to help other women. *Women need to step into their non-comfort zone and ask for help* is my mantra. Now hold on before you send me a nasty e-mail about all this; know I agree us as women should help each other triumph, but I prefer looking at mentoring and leadership as the best person getting the job, not the best body part.

Realize you may have to pay to play. In certain avenues mentors are just not available, such as entrepreneurs or small businesses. Mentors may not be easy to find. You may need to hire a mentor/coach. Approach this from a business head versus a heart's wallet. Often the fee charge for coaching is reimbursable from your organization as well as a tax write-off under professional development. Keep in the back of your mind that a great mentor/coach can be a bit expensive as you get what you pay for.

Look where you least expect to find a mentor. A good

mentor is not defined by where they work. You may find a mentor in a professional association, networking group, or via friend of a friend. Keep your eyes open.

When you find the right mentor, be sure you are focused on work, not outside garbage. Be humble; this is about helping you not showing off. There should be no judgment in a mentor relationship. This is where you can come and share your mistakes. Confidentiality is just as important in this relationship as they, the mentor, will be sharing information not for general consumption. I have fired mentees for this, where I have shared an idea only to see it blogged about a month later by my mentee. Remember to have fun and celebrate your gains!

Chapter 7

She's Not Just a Pretty Face
Creating the Female Bridge

A bridge is the fundamental structure that links our past to our future, mistakes to lessons and the fallen to success. Women need to build a better bridge today if they want to thrive tomorrow.

Why Can't We All Just Get Along

The only person you can change is yourself...all others will follow If they don't—it's their loss.

Women are very unique creatures. We have a tendency towards empathy and compassion, love and emotion, and when it comes to children, we tend to have the protection instinct of a mother bear. Yet when it comes to other women...well, we can just be downright mean. Now I know some argue our behavior is evolution based—we as women tend to go after the strongest hunter in a tribe. However, I am not sure I was looking for a hunter—or breadwinner for that matter. And others argue women have a tendency to just be jealous creatures, being petty when another woman has a "better" lifestyle than the one they have. Some even argue this nastiness is societal based. Still more say that television, magazines, and social media display and endorse nastiness as a strength for women. Hey, just look at the reality shows now on the tube. Whatever the reason, however, the only way we can change this behavior is by changing our own.

So Let's Stop this Battle

Would not it be wonderful if I could just wave a wand and end the "us versus us" battles women seem to avail themselves to? Imagine where you could place all that new-found energy? Rather than looking at another and seeing what you want to see, why not sit back and wait before passing a judgment? Ask yourself what that judgment says about you. And if she has fallen, rather than handing her the thorny side of a rose, offer a hand to help her up, without judgment.

SHIFTING PARADIGMS

Recently while attending a rather large holiday get together with several women, "Kim" decided, for whatever reason, she would weigh in on a couple who was attending. The couple was dating and Kim decided this was a good time to make an off-the-cuff, nasty remark about the woman this gentleman was dating. Kim had no idea if this woman "Tracy" had any friends in the group and quite honestly did not care. The comment was rude and distasteful.

Now ladies, we know the comment had nothing to do with Tracy—it was all about Kim's insecurity and thus made Kim look like an %&$#! However, the comment did make a few uncomfortable. I would even go as far as to say this comment may bias those who did not know Tracy at this point.

Think about how you would handle this now that you have read this section. Would you confront Kim, tell Tracy, or just walk away? Me being me, and how I love conflict, I would confront Kim—but out of ear shot of everyone else. I would let her know I was concerned about her and that her comment only reflected other "stuff" is going on with Kim.

In the business world, this message gets even more skewed as I have often heard comments "well she should mentor me, she is a woman and it is her duty to other women to mentor other women," "she slept her way to the top," and much more colorful content. How does this comment sit with you: "Women in leadership appear to fall into two categories— a bitch or a pushover with no skill." Shocker, yes. I hate how strong women are perceived and how judgment is being passed by other women. It happens in the boardroom, lunch room and then bleeds into the home life with social groups.

With all the thought leadership on women helping women achieve, you would think they would address the nastiness first. Call it for what it is: bullshit!

You may not agree with another woman, but to criticize her appearance—as opposed to her ideas or action—isn't doing anyone favors, least of all you.

Hillary Rodham Clinton,
Former United States Secretary of State, U.S. Senator, and First Lady of the United States

So I challenge you to stop looking at others with green or rose colored glasses. To truly see the beauty each woman/person offers to the world. To place the nasty where it belongs: in the garbage, as you are a role model for all around you. If there is someone you care not to befriend, that is fine— just walk away. And if you are the one they are gossiping about...

Do not give up any cake to them. They just wish they were you.

This next section dives into taking control and moving forward with women on your side. We examine a few hot debates as well as tools and tips to get you ahead.

After all, we are **ALL** charged with creating the female bridge.

The Gift of Motherhood

Motherhood is a wonderful gift however don't lose yourself in that gift.

As women, we have a plethora of decisions that determine our career and life paths. These decisions start at a very young age and do not end. Today I still face many of these decisions. Those decisions include: what college we attend, degree, marriage, military, career aspirations, personal aspirations, and of course the big one: family. Decisions are pathways for us, and while some may define a part of us, the whole is still yet undetermined. So how do we become more than a title? One of the greatest strengths women have from our own gender determination is multitasking and being more than just one thing. It is hard wired in our brain to be able to just be more.

The battle of motherhood rages on today more so then in any other generation of our past and it appears –however I disagree – motherhood today is failing. In a recent large national survey of motherhood by Pew Research Center (n.d.2007), the vast majority (56%) stated they believed today's moms are failing as compared to say twenty years ago. Add to that, 38% felt the biggest risk to today's youth is external influences. To add fuel to this fire, an overwhelming agreement (70%) of women felt the role of motherhood today is more challenging than that of our parents resulting to a whopping 80% claiming Generational X's mothering style is worse than the Baby-boomers style. OUCH! The rationale as to the why we are failing so miserably, according to the study, falls to external influences, social media, dual working-parent households and lack of social supports.

With statistics like this, I ask why we then battle other moms instead of uniting with them.

When I started writing this chapter, I found myself going from the angle of us versus them; stay at home versus return to work. Yes, I was writing this chapter as part of the problem, not a chapter based on solution. Even the title changed from the Battle of Motherhood to The Gift of Motherhood. I share this because I want you to understand we all are growing and learning. If we are part of the problem, we cannot find the solution. In the smallest shift of perspective, where one looks a bit deeper and asks, does this help or hurt, growth occurs.

More than a Mom and the Battlefield_____

I often find it funny how women, who scream for equality, right out of the gate compare motherhood/parenting styles versus those of other women. When is it enough to be a mom? Why do we feel we need to compete with each other over those who stay at home versus those who return to work? Guess what? We are our worst enemy.

Shortly after the birth of our son, struggling with a touch of postpartum, I struggled with breast-feeding. Our son, all 11 pounds of him (at birth) was starving, and thus...yes, sleep deprived, blue, and in need of a glass of wine, I caved in and decided the bottle was our best option. This decision was not made lightly and I was already feeling a tad bit guilty. To my amazement, I often heard from my fellow mothers how I was letting my son down by going to the bottle. I even had a close friend—not a mom herself, mind you—offer to teach me how to breast-feed. Now, I am not about to go off on bottle versus breast-feeding, but in the end...keep your opinion to yourself. This is not a competition.

This banter still continues, and I am sure I will receive a few e-mails to my comment above, but once the child hits twelve weeks the bottle debate goes to the wayside as we now focus on the Parenting 101 question: to work or not to work. And both sides feel equally knowledgeable to weigh in on what is best for the woman, her family, and her child.

Trust me when I add, when I decided to return to work after our son was born, it was the hardest decision I ever made. The first day of daycare I sat in the parking lot for three hours crying. It was another mother, sitting in my car, who just listened to me. She let me cry—she affirmed I was not a bad mom, that the tears were normal as she too cried. This is the beauty of womanhood and the selfless gifts we give others.

THE MISNOMERS

So let me clear the air and toss some misnomers out so we are all on the same page and we can put these battles to rest:

Motherhood is NOT a thankless job.

Regardless of whether you work or not, motherhood is rewarding. My children thank me hundreds of ways. You just have to open your eyes to them. If you believe being a mom is thankless, you are not looking hard enough to see the wonderful gift in front of you. When was the last time we heard a father stating "fatherhood is a thankless job"—and please let's not argue it is, because they are not responsible for childcare. Yes my readers, that comment is a scapegoat. My husband is equally responsible for everything my children need, want and do.

When one of our children decided it was naked day at school and managed to get everyone in class to strip down (it took all of 3 minutes while the teacher had her head turned), we both were called in—and we both reveled in the joy of that child (she takes after me).

When our son's soccer team wins a game—I coached these amazing young men, what a team (goose bumps)—I celebrated with my entire family for the win. My husband, who sits on the sideline cheering away, is just as much a part of the team as I am. It is not me and you, it is a parenting "us." I may be the coach, but he is the support that allows me to coach. He also is my eyes and ears on the sidelines.

Staying at home with your child is one of the toughest jobs a woman or man can ever have.

I love that we are starting to see men staying home, not because "we are women and hear us roar," but because I love that they are allowing themselves to embrace the gift of fatherhood and that they can spend more time with their children. I love that they are man enough to step aside and let their other half lead for a while in the workplace. I love that they recognize staying at home does not define them or their masculinity.

When our twins were born, we decided I would stay home and raise all three children. I love being a mom, but staying home nearly cost me my sanity. I can see how some lose themselves in all their children do. It is overwhelming, and there is a complete loss of time control as you no longer have your schedule. Honestly, for me, it was leading a team that need more than a leader—they needed a mom and that entailed EVERYTHING I HAD. Add to that, to keep my sanity, I started a small home wine tasting company just for adult connections (and wine), joined a large town moms' group—where unfortunately I did not fit in (my choice)—and began volunteering.

When you are staying at home, boundaries get blurred as often "we" feel we need to do everything. Hey, I was right there doing everything: all the cleaning, cooking, childcare, medical needs, social needs, playdates etc. When women stay home, I think we forget we are still part of a partnership. We forget that we can ask for help—and if you do not ask for that help, you get overburdened. You have to give yourself permission to ask for help. We cannot do it all, nor should we. What lesson are we teaching our children or other women for that matter?

I was fortunate: one of my close friends, Maria (also a mom but who returned to work), would often remind me to ask for help...even from her. She is part of my support network. She is there for me and my family and me her. We help each other out when the need arises. I also learned how to ask for help.

Staying at home with the children does not equate to brain mush unless YOU let it.

You have a choice to stay current with your passion, live through your children, or allow your own self to hide. It is all on you—you own this decision. Shift your perspective from staying at home rearing children to an opportunity to find where your passion now lies. I state "now lies" because as we get older, our focus and needs shift, and so do passions. The Internet is your highway to knowledge—not social media. Stop wasting time playing games and start focusing on YOU. You decide if you wish to take care of you or not. You decided what you eat...sleep...when to exercise or not.

In my early twenties I found a love for red wine, but life kind of got in the way. When I decided to stay at home with my kids that passion returned (and not for drinking it!). I began reading all about the different varieties of grapes, regions, brix mixes, and more. I created a vision board of where I wanted to go and what I wanted to try in regards to wine. I kept my brain engaged in a passion of learning mode. I also decided to return to school and achieve my Master's degree in Organizational Psychology. Believe it or not, this passion for ongoing learning is now fostering itself in my children as they still see me reading, learning and growing. In taking care of me, I in turn take care of them.

Returning to work does not make you a bad mom, make you selfish, or damage the kids.

This battle seems to still rage, and I often believe the media is in large part a factor in fueling the flames. I am amazed how many articles I could find about this topic and the views from both sides. Is it the fact that some women do not define themselves in staying at home or have found work they are passionate about? I cannot tell you how many women have apologized to me for my returning to work. The return to work was my choice—not because I was selfish or wanted to damage my kids—it was because what I do gives me goose bumps. My career is part of what makes Lauran Star...Lauran Star. Yes, I found my passion sweet spot, and you can find yours too.

In fact women who return to work tend to have a higher self-esteem and independence than those who stay home (Wattis, et al., 2013), regardless of how many hours they work. That's right: you get this benefit if you work five or forty hours. Working nights, however, can lend itself to a bit more stress as the needs of the family during the day carry into the night. Returning to work can be for hundreds of reasons ranging from financial to personal. There also appears to be greater home life harmony as women who work tend to see work and family as separate entities—thus they tend to be more present when in the family world.

I myself know I am a better mom because I work. In large part, I love that my children see me as both a mom and a fulfilled business woman. I like the financial security my employment brings, and that I can go do lunch with my friends when I want. I am happier when I am working than when I am not. Does that mean my house is not spotless 24/7? Sure, but neither is yours. If this makes me selfish, too bad! That is your opinion, and more than likely we are not friends, so your opinion means nothing to me. You see, I have the ultimate choice in the value of your opinion—not you.

When I look at whom I care about, I am blessed to have a wide range of friends. Some are moms, some not, some work and others do not, and guess what: neither path is the easiest or the best. Neither family structure nor kids are grander. All are unique, regardless of where they are in their career or life choices. We are friends because we call it like we see it, care and are there for each other and we accept each other as we are.

Working parents do in fact have less time to volunteer, but they do their share of volunteering.

The recent data supports both working and non-working parents volunteer equal amounts of time. Here is the kicker: look around and see who is volunteering. It tends to be the same people—moms and dads—and they volunteer in large part because they want to. It gives them cake.

We need to stop thinking of motherhood as an *us versus them* mentality. Ask yourself, why are you volunteering and who does it benefit? If you do not volunteer, ask yourself, why? Look for opportunities that inspire you i.e., if you love reading, volunteer to go in and read. I am passionate about empowering the youth, thus my volunteering has been on the soccer and lacrosse field. I see youth coaching as a wonderful way to empower all to thrive. The funny part is, all I l know about both sports comes from a book. That's right, I never played either. Yet I can inspire, so I surround myself with others who know the game. At the end of the day, if you are happy, then so be it.

There is such a thing as Motherhood Burnout.

Does any of the following sound familiar?

- You have no idea what your passion is.
- If the kids are not involved you lose interest.
- Being a mom is all you are, even if you work.

- You no longer care about what you look like…"hey I showered today."
- Finger food is eating off your kid's plate for all three meals—because chicken nuggets are yummy.
- When you go to a restaurant you believe you deserve the kid menu too because that is where the mac n cheese is.
- Sex…what the hell is that?
- Your spouse is the guy who comes home at night and watches TV.

Motherhood Burnout is when a mom just gets lost in the role and no longer can find herself or happiness. It can happen to both the stay at home and return-to- work parent. This burnout can devastate you and your family in large part because as moms we are the lynchpin of the family. If we do not take care of that pin, the whole family can fall apart. Moms are the next generation role models (like you needed another function). Your children will follow in your footsteps.

How to overcome this: take some "me time." Now, I know that is easier said than done, but if you look at where you are spending your time (cake), you now may see some opportunities for you time.

In the end, let's look at our similarities as mothers, not our differences, and embrace each other. Mothers are special as we have an unfathomable amount of love, not just for our own children—it includes all that our children touch and meet. If you need to dig deep to see the beauty of a different style of parenting, then do so—for you are responsible for the next generation of amazing women. They learn who they are, how they respond and react, and how to care from you. Their inner beauty is a direct reflection of your parenting.

Raising the Next Generation of Leaders

Cheers to the current and next generation of amazing leaders! How are you helping them grow?

My Amazing 3/4th Town Champions Girls Soccer!

When I am not speaking, writing or teaching, you can find me on the soccer and lacrosse fields empowering girls and boys. I coach youth girls Lacrosse and youth boys and girls soccer. The funny part is, I learned all about both sports from books and videos—you see, I don't have an athletic bone in my body. However, this does not define me, as the girls above are town champions, and I hold several town team championships. The titles mean nothing compared to the lessons I am teaching on the field—teamwork, getting along, helping each other, having each other's back, and the most important lesson: You can do anything if you want it bad enough. I love my players; their desire to play and have fun is amazing, and I'm proud of how they communicate and problem solve in the simplest forms. The point: it does not take a ton of skill to mentor the next generation—it does take passion.

As women today, our role, much like our parents, is raising the next generation of leaders. We do this both at home and at work. It is important to recognize the approach may be different from children to adults; however, the end results are usually the same: an engaged and resilient workforce. Let us look at them both.

THE PLAYGROUND

Regardless if you have children or not, your actions in the business world shape their perception. Some of our greatest role models go unsung, as these individuals never ask for the rewards—they see the results of what they are doing.

Thank you to the countless teachers, college professors, coaches, and mentors that helped shaped me to be who I am. Thank you to my parents, who did the best they could— however flawed it was—that shaped my inner strength to overcome the negative situations. Thank you to all those who are now helping to shape my daughters and my son.

In raising the next generation of leaders in our children, gender does not matter as much. Our children are learning they can be whomever they wish to be, and gender, class or ethnic boundaries do not hold them back. Now, if that statement made you cringe a bit or roll your eyes, I have to ask...are you part of the problem or part of the solution? Are you, yourself, allowing the above to hold you back? Are you teaching the next generation that it is OK to allow the stereotypes to hold them back by giving them power to define who they are? Or are you letting go of the ill of the past, thus embracing the lesson?

Recently on the playground I overheard an African American child tell a Caucasian child it was his fault his daddy lost his job. The two children continued to play, but I was a bit shocked by this statement, and yes, being me, I decided to investigate. I found this child's mom sitting on a park bench. When I mentioned the comment, she stated it was true—the white man has always held her kind back.... Now, I could have spent hours hoping to enlighten this individual on the number of job losses in the United States, or how the past might be skewing her perspective, but one needs to be open to grow.

Children are sponges, they absorb everything. They are aware who is in their corner and who could care less. They observe and then repeat what they see. I argue if we truly wish to end prejudices, we need to start at home. A child who only learns rewards come from good behavior will fall short when asked to take risks.

There are countless books on childrearing but very few on mentoring, in large part because we seem to assume once you are a parent you have Emotional Intelligence. Emotional Intelligence (EI) is how we relate to those around us, and while this book is not focused on EI, it is important to note the greater need for understanding self-awareness and behavioral awareness. We grew up with the "do as I say not as I do" mentality...not shocking it did not work. In being self- aware you can begin to understand how your actions affect those around you, including the little people everywhere.

SHIFTING PARADIGMS

If we are to be judge as to how we raise our children and help the elderly, then why are we not helping the next generation or current with our current knowledge and success? Identify your strong points—things you can teach or empower others with. Find ways to do so. It may be running a webinar or tele class, or one-on-one conversation. It does no one any good if the aptitude you have today is not gifted tomorrow.

Our emerging workforce is not interested in command-and-control leadership. They don't want to do things because I said so; they want to do things because they want to do them.

Irene Rosenfeld,
CEO of Mondelēz International

SOME WAYS TO INSPIRE IN THE WORKPLACE_____

Give the opportunity to shine. Regardless of age, creating opportunities for your underlings empowers them to step into the lime light, shine, and then learn how to take a bow and keep their personal power, versus giving it away. In the same light, show them also how you can shine. Demonstrate how to bask in the glory rather than giving the light away—when it is your due.

Encourage sharing of information. This is a knowhow skill we all must master. Keeping an open dialogue both at work or wherever engagements happen allows both you and them to grow through past experience. Both bring unique talents to the table. Explore and learn together.

Be open about failure. Gen Y's struggle with failure; they do not know how to process it or learn from it, thus it has become our role to show them how through risk taking, failing is an acceptable loss. Then create action steps to inspire resilience. Show them how you pick yourself up, dust off and then learn from the experience. Provide a safety net for learning where mistakes are a fact of life. It is how we handle those blunders.

Provide constructive feedback versus criticism. The difference between the two is feedback has positive action steps and criticism comes with blame. Regardless of who you are, feedback is craved. We all want to know what we are doing well and how we can adapt and improve. Constructive feedback is showing me the how and why, criticism is the what.

Pivot your biases. That is correct, with the next generation already in the workforce our own personal biases are tainting how we raise them. See the positive in what they bring versus the negative.

Be open to learn. In sharing your knowledge, expect them to share theirs. Remember whomever you are raising up, they too have something to offer you. Wisdom is a two-way street.

Listen to what they are saying. More often than not, we tend to place our conversational needs first only to then learn what we were planning on sharing has nothing to do with the situation at hand. Learn to listen; you may be surprised at what you hear.

To heck with comfort zone. Being uncomfortable develops out-of-the-box thinkers—encourage it.

Be a role model and approachable.

Building a bridge today in the workplace is equally as important as it was, say, twenty years ago, but with more women in the workplace today, more attention is paid to this. Here is the kicker: if we do not help the next generation then history will repeat itself. It is like doing the tango; one step forward one step back. And it is not gender specific.

Chapter 8
Getting fired with style.
The exit strategy

In the face of adversity, it is not the reason of such rival but how we handle ourselves that people remember.

You're Fired...with Style

If you do not see it coming...you need to work on Self and Organizational Awareness.

I have been proudly terminated twice in my life—well, three times if you count the time my own mother fired me. That being said, I learned the most from my reaction to being fired rather than the process itself. Losing a job is almost a rite of passage. Regardless of the reason, how you bounce back and what you grasp during this time shapes how you approach your next career move. Being terminated is not like being rejected in a relationship, you cannot select the next position poorly and then chalk it up to the infamous rebound effect. Every move you make after termination can be scrutinized by your next employer and even further after that.

The first time I was terminated, I was caught off guard. Shame on me, as I should have seen it coming. I was prohibited to interview for advancement due to my gender. I was fully aware of this and in contact with an attorney at the time. I had even filed a claim with the Equal Opportunity Commission in my current state. Yet, under the guise I was due for a performance appraisal, when I went in to meet with my supervisor—SLAM. I even brought the jerk coffee. DUH. Why else would they be meeting with me? Never mind that human resources was present. In the back of my mind, I knew termination might happen; however, in my emotional mind I was thinking "they would never fire me, I am Lauran Star. Not only that, it would be retaliation termination, a huge NO-NO pending my EOC claim." So there I sat, dumbfounded. I had to have them repeat it to me three times…"You're firing me? No seriously, you are terminating me?" Looking back today, I must have appeared as naive and shocked as I felt. It was not in that moment that I learned anything as my emotions took over, sabotaging any and all thoughts. Days later, however, I found myself depressed and shocked, asking myself: *What would I do now, how would I find a job, who do I contact, am I worthy of another placement, is this the right field for me anymore?*

Adversity awakens in us a strong will to a daring life.
You become a stronger person with each adversity that you
overcome.

Lailah Gifty Akita

Does this sound familiar? When the loss of a position hits, we still need to grieve, even if the position was not the right fit or your growth was stumped. It can take months to rebound back, and this is where the schooling begins on how to get fired with style.

In the end, once I pulled myself out of my pity party (hey, everyone loves a good pity party now and then), I had several decisions to make and questions to ask. The biggest one of them all was *What to do next and how did this happen?* I found myself deeply looking inward to see why I decided to put my career in sales leadership on the line. What was it, besides being discriminated against, that caused and then dictated my action? I had to examine what motivated me to do what I did and I would do it again.

I decided getting fired was the single best thing that could have happened to my career in sales. I had already done it all in the sales leadership spectrum—you see, I stopped growing. Therefore, my actions were out of boredom and a need to make some noise. To the question of would I take the same actions that I did again... the answer HELL YES. I saw a gross incompetence in the organization where women leadership should have been thriving however due to past biases and lack of knowledge it was not. I had to do something and yes I am very glad I did.

Now, I had a unique opportunity to re-invest in my career dreams. A chance to repaint my canvas anew in a field that fulfills me. From this termination the real Lauran Star came to be. I recognized what truly motivates me. The powerhouse, not to be messed with, empowering other women to thrive, enjoying work because I can, and loving life to the fullest type of person. I found my career self in that termination.

Remember, I mentioned I was terminated twice, and so yes, the next time I lost my position/contract I was very much more prepared. The conversation went along the lines of, Company A: "At this time Lauran we need to terminate our engagement with you" Lauran Star: "Well that is unfortunate. I wish you all the best of luck, bye-bye." Why the vast difference? I saw this coming and I had an exit strategy. I remembered it was business not personal. And while I still mourned the loss of this commitment, the grieving period was very short. Hell, I already had opportunities in place.

No matter how you exit an organization, be it gainfully employed (professional career) or owning a business (entrepreneurial), through termination, quitting, promotion or layoffs, it is critical to have a solid exit strategy.

The truth will set you free. But first, it will piss you off.

Gloria Steinem

LESSONS OF BEING FIRED…TWICE_____

Lessons learned are better off not repeated. What did I learn from my termination? First off, I have to pony up and take on accountability for my part. I had to introspect what I would have done differently or not changed.

- **Fault:** Where was I at fault? Let us just say it: if you are terminated, you had a hand in it. I learned I was and still am a bit outspoken—although I like to call it rakish and provocative.

- **Responsibility:** I was also reminded no matter how good I am – I am one hundred percent responsible for my actions. I think we sometimes forget this especially in an atmosphere where your focus is in goal attainment verses emotional intelligence in the workspace.

- **Friend or Foe**: I discovered who my allies truly were and who were not – this is important as you need to go find other contracts or employment.

- **Their memory**: No one remembers why you are terminated however EVERYONE remember how you handled it. I had to learn who my true connections were. As I am sure gossip spreads throughout a company like jelly on peanut butter, it became very clear who had my back. These are my keeper contacts in an organization

- **Money**: I also learned the importance of financial planning. While data suggests you should have at least six months of salary saved, I can tell you, you will need more. Fortunately my husband is very fiscally responsible (thank God one of us is). While we had to make cutbacks, today I am prepared for anything.

- ***So they don't like me***: Too bad - so sad. You need to separate your own value from your work value. They are not the same.

- ***Listen to my Gut:*** From the start with both positions where as I was terminated, I never felt it was a career move rather they were both just jobs. Even in the interviewing process I knew this was short term. I should have listened to my instincts and passed from the get go.

- ***One glass of wine***: It is okay to grieve providing you are mourning the job loss not your own skills. Keep it focused on what is real and what is not. If I need more than one glass of wine to get over the job/contract loss something else is going on and more often than not it is my accountability issue of the reason of termination. It is hard to face the truth however it is also very freeing.

Getting fired was not the end of the world, in fact just the opposite, as it opened a new door. Believe it or not, some terminations are a sign you just outgrew the company and this is business way of pushing you further – if you let it.

Networking is like a stream, it is constantly moving.

I had to learn how to network all over again. Social media kicks my end in large part because it is not second nature to me or my generation. I still work on this, but there are days I win. In recreating myself, I did not have to walk the walk of endless interview; nevertheless I did stay current with my own techniques. Times have changed. This position I had I found in the newspaper. Hmm...do they even print those anymore?

Welcome Exit Strategy

An exit strategy is a backup plan in case termination, layoff or promotions are in your future. The economic market today is stronger than it was say five years ago, where businesses were quick to fire. Today, employees are noting they feel a bit safer in their current position, but the risk of job loss is still present. I believe it is prudent to have two exit plans of action in place: one for promotions and the other for termination.

Promotions:

You have been with the company a few years, done an excellent job and are starting to get noticed. It is time, in your opinion, to start to climb the old ladder. First step is organizational awareness. Organizational awareness is the understanding of how leadership and an organization functions and performs, along with its abilities, potential, and results. It is a clear understanding of how the sub group or departments function under the organizational umbrella. It is knowing the *who, what, when,* and *where* of peers, departments, management, and the organization. It is gaining a better perspective of the organization's departmental mission, political flavor, and allies. Outside the organization some call this "intuition." I like to call all this "being in the know." If you are not in the know, get there. Ask for an org chart of who is who. Uncover who gets things done and then find way to link with that person. Once you have the lay of the land, begin to uncover where you wish to go next.

- *What is your next step within the company/business*? If you are working for an organization, what is your next promotion? Is it clearly defined? Who do you need to know? Whom does it report to? What skills or requirements are needed?
- *Are you on the fast track for a promotion*? It is imperative you know where you fall in your chain of success. Are you at the top or near the bottom? Who is ahead of you and why? What skills do you need or are lacking? Whose ear do you have, and whose ear do they have?
- *What does your professional/business one-year plan look like?* Success does not just happen, smart women

make it happen by planning for it.

- **Who is in your corner/networks?** Are you a member of LinkedIn and focused in your area of expertise or do you just "play"? This can be a make or break factor between getting a new stream of revenue today versus nine months from now.

- **Who can help you find the next step?** Have a go-to list of contacts that can make recommendations, referrals, and help you land the next big thing for yourself.

- **Where do you currently stand within your company or business?** Often when employees lose a promotion it is in large part because of poor organizational/business-awareness. This is followed by a lack of SMART goals. If you are falling short here when creating your exit strategy, find a mentor or coach to help you.

Write this plan down and keep it where you can modify it when you need to. For promotions it is not enough to just know where you are going; you need to write it down.

TERMINATION/LAYOFF

Terminations result first in an emotional response. It is natural as no one likes rejection, but having high self and behavioral awareness will help you get through this transition.

Having a plan also provides a bit of emotional support as you are not left feeling totally vulnerable.

- ***If you are terminated today, where will you go?*** Do you have connections and networks in place to get you moving? Who are they? Create a list NOW.
- ***What did you learn?*** Yes, even in termination there is growth. However, you have to truly self-reflect to find the reasons. I have yet to hear of an employee who was 100 percent innocent of the termination. Termination is a great place for professional and personal growth— trust me on that.
- ***How long can you take to find gainful employment (savings)?*** The average savings should be more than six months of your salary—no kidding. What would you need to liquidate should you lose revenue tomorrow? What is the least amount of money you need weekly to survive? Start saving now.
- ***Who is in your corner/networks?*** Are you a member of LinkedIn and focused in your area of expertise or do you just "play"? This can be a make or break between getting a new stream of revenue today versus nine months from now. What new markets should you be playing in (sandboxes)?
- ***Who can help you find the next step?*** Have a go-to list

of contacts that can make recommendations, referrals, and help you land the next big thing for yourself.

- **Where do you currently stand within your company or business?** Often when employees or entrepreneurs lose their income/job, it is in large part because of poor organizational/business-awareness. This is followed by a lack of SMART goals. If you are falling short here when creating your exit strategy, find a mentor or coach to help you.

- **Is your resume up to date?** You should update your resume yearly and keep a WAY TO GO file of all awards, recommendations, sales numbers, profit statements, etc.

- **What companies look good to you?** I am constantly checking out companies I find interesting. I make a list of who's who, and then yes, connect with them on LinkedIn or other social media sites.

- **What have you done for me lately?** Be sure you are giving as much as you get. I hate getting a call from someone once they are in need of something and it's the only reason they called.

- **How long will you allow yourself to grieve?** This is a reasonable question, as a loss of a job or business is a loss all the same. If you have in your mind well before the length of time you are allowed to wallow, you will recover more quickly.

- ***What makes you marketable?*** That's right, what make you so special?

You know the person who gets fired and has a job 48 hours later? Yup, they have a solid executable termination plan. To that point they are also working it. If you examine all the bullets above, you probably can see how they can benefit you today rather than waiting until a downsizing. One thing they all have in common is keeping you current in networking. Discovering new employment today is so different from yesterday—and tomorrow, who knows what will be new. From job boards to recruits, the one single reoccurring theme in successful job hunting is connections.

How to Get Fired with Style

All right, the moment is here and you may or may not have seen it coming. Being terminated is part of work history, so put your big girl panties on and now let's leave with class.

Breathe. One of the biggest mistakes we make when being faced with any fear is that we forget to breathe. In termination our emotions hijack our brain and thus we have all seen it: screaming, tears, yelling, threats, and drama. I am not immune, as that was how I reacted the first time I was let go. I too, forgot to breathe and take a moment.

Let it go. For whatever reason, we partially believe we can talk our way into being kept. When that moment comes a verdict already has been made. We are also too vulnerable to make any sound arguments. No matter what you say at that moment, they are not going to change their minds. Think about it: the process of termination is not up to one person; in most cases a manager, supervisor, and human resources were all notified. There is a chain of command that needs to be addressed, and by showing they are wrong does not shine well for you—at that moment.

Leave on your terms. Your first thoughts should be the terms of the discontinuation of employment. What does severance look like, what do you keep in terms of equipment, vacation or sick days, 401K, stock options, and benefits. While most of this is a standard package, feel free to negotiate. Being prepared for the rainy day is the best approach. I was unprepared the first time I was let go, but in the second, I rode the horse. I had written all this down in my first week of employment. I call this my *In the event of my unfortunate termination* letter. I clearly list what I wanted to be sure I kept.

Smile and Wave gals...Smile and Wave. This is not the time to start plotting revenge. Leave with your head high and remember it is their loss and your gain (although you may feel like you just got kicked in the stomach). Grab your gear and walk out of the office. The office loves gossip—do not give them any. Leave them all wondering what you know and they don't.

Lawyer if needed. Give yourself 72 hours of head-clearing space, and then decide if the termination was just or not. Most states in the United States are Employee at Will states, meaning the curtain can close for any reason except if you are a protected class, in retaliation for whistle blowing or anything discriminatory.

Shut off social media. The world is your stage, but stay off it for at least three days. Do not post, tweet, link, anything. There seems to be a draw to post a picture of yourself having a great time somewhere just after termination...hmm, what does that say?

Pivotal Women:
Vicky Oliver, Career Specialist and author of **301 Smart Answers to Tough Interview Questions** (Sourcebooks, 2005)
How do you address your termination in an interview?

If you've ever been fired or let go, you should expect the topic will come up in an interview. Even if the layoff happened several jobs before your current one, you should be prepared to answer all sorts of questions about your termination. But knowing that the topic *will* surface also gives you a chance to prepare. Work out your explanation and practice it.

First: there is a difference between being laid off and fired. A layoff means you were pink-slipped along with many others in your organization during the same time period. If you were laid off, you want to position it in the best possible light. Figure out the number of other workers who also lost their jobs. Sometimes it will work to your advantage to talk in terms of percentages— i.e. "20% of the workforce was cut." Other times, the number of people will sound higher, i.e. "100 people were cut," in which case, use *that* statistic.

Just be sure that whatever you say is accurate. A big layoff carries little stigma. Just be sure to sound professional about it, and provide some background for probable reasons why you were one of the unfortunate ones.

If you were fired, that means you lost your job for cause. You need to be forthright about it, and say what you learned from the experience. Never ever bad mouth anyone whom you worked for. Discuss lessons learned and what you will carry forward from the experience. The way you discuss a past termination can make or break your chances of getting hired again. Practice how you will address this vital topic with a job-hunting buddy, and good luck!

Getting Back in the Saddle Again

*No matter the cause, getting in the saddle again can be rear
staking painful
Yet, heart-filling powerful.*

Sometimes life gets in the way of our career paths; it is what makes life wonderful and yet again challenging. In the face of today's workplace, women lead men over taking time off and it is no wonder—from aging parents to childbirth, women are the focal point of most American families. We are the information center, the care takers, the multitaskers and the do-it-all-ers. And when all is done, we then make that decision: do we return to work, and how.

Regardless of the reason for leaving the workforce, there are a few falsehoods that need to be addressed before we can slide into how to return to the workforce.

Motherhood will set your career on the slow track

Starting a family is a huge decision couples do not take lightly. Family life, for the most part, is as choice, and while many will have you believe motherhood will set your career on the slow track, I disagree. I believe, much like the glass ceiling, motherhood can become a scapegoat for slow advancement rather than the real fact that advancement is a choice. While out on maternity leave, our perspective often shifts to what is truly important—or more to the point, is it quality or quantity of life that we seek? I recently read an article on how men benefit from children while women suffer; this article was solely based on one woman's plight in the workforce, not research or statistical differences. As informed consumers in this social media day and age, we need to be better researchers. We need to dig a bit deeper. Yes, we are the nurturers and caretakers, the CEOs of our households, the medical people, cleaners, cooks, and the decision makers. When we are faced with the choice to return to the workforce, we also are the primary decision makers in childcare placement. We also make a choice, all too often, to forgo our career for the family.

Women returning to work after an extended leave of absence receive reduced titles

There are some who argue that if you leave employment as a leader, you should return as one. I agree; however, it is not as simple as saying "I was a leader yesterday, thus I deserve to be a leader today." In understanding these questions, you will gain a better appreciation of the leadership role at your organization and how to climb the wall faster.

Evaluating how long you are away from your employment provides insight into your protection of title. The FMLA

(Family Medical Leave Act) provides job protection for both men and women who take a leave of absence up to twelve weeks for family or medical reasons. However, there are several loop holes in the FMLA; check with your company in regards to how they apply this act.

However, it is not all lost, as we still can go back if we so choose...yet typically not at the same level. Does this surprise you? It shouldn't, as many things may have changed while you were away from your desk. Yet all too often, we do expect it and get upset if we are not right back on the horse as if we never left.

Thus, if you are returning to work from any long period of time off (more than six months), you need to ask the following questions of yourself and of the market:

- What is important to you today? Be honest with yourself as your motivation may have shifted towards intrinsic values versus extrinsic (car, money, titles). What has changed in you? Family, career aspirations, work/life balance, education level.
- What are you willing to give up by returning to work? I believe women can certainly have it all, but not all at the same time. This is realistic.
- What has changed in the career role? Has technology moved forward, are the client's needs the same, can the

organization deliver to the client or are there obstacles, does the role have new guidelines and tasks? How will you address these changes or stay current while out on leave?

- What are the new factors affecting your career choices? Is there a new method to the organizations structure, what does the job economy look like today, NOT yesterday, what does this career choice future look like?

- What are today's leaders facing that yesterday's leaders were not? How has the leadership landscape changed? (Trust me it has.) What do you need skill wise and emotional intelligence wise to cope with these changes?

- How will your leader emerge and benefit the organization once you return to work?

- What new skills do you bring into the workforce? Where did you grow while on leave? What new aspirations do you have?

SETTING YOURSELF UP FOR SUCCESS_____

What we understand about leaves of absence may surprise you. Thus, being a bit more prepared may make your entry back into the workplace a greater success. Studies show (Wiese et al. 2012) women with high emotional stability and preparedness for reentry into the workplace are less likely to regret their choice to return. They are ready and have the family support needed to move forward with their career. We also recognize that a shorter leave of absence, especially in light of a dying parent or child birth, can result in greater stress. Put yourself first and take the time you need; you will be a greater asset to those around you. Be sure you are completely ready to return to the demands of the workplace.

Lauran Star

Chapter 9

This Is Your Time...
What Will You Do With It

At the end of your life the one thing we want more of is time. Use it wisely.

Lauran Star

Keeping Your Personal Power

In every struggle it comes down to personal power and your choice, to keep it or hand it over.

What is Personal Power?

This is the ability to get what you desire in a tactful way. It is the overall ability to assert yourself in any situation and then maneuver the situation into a win/win resolution for all involved. It also is a visible and visceral, strong inner calm. It is the inner belief that you are in charge of your life and can accomplish anything you want, if you want it badly enough. It also is the ability to let go of those things you cannot control or wish not to control.

Personal power has little to do with positional power, that is, where you rank in an organization, class system, or life. I have worked with several high ranking officials that lack this skill and yet found it in children. It is also very easily identified, as women who have this talent are like magnets. We all want to hang with them. They march to their own music and code of ethics. They change their lives whenever need be.

Note this as a skill as it is an Emotional Intelligence proficiency, and like a muscle, use it or loss it.

Children have immeasurable amounts of personal

power—they do not know any better. I love how much power I see on a daily basis from my own kids, and I strive to keep it in place. As a parent, one of my values is to empower my own children to be themselves and live in their strengths. I work hard both in school and in sports, letting all who have an impact know that risks and mistakes are a good thing, that the glass is full and if you empty my child's glass, you better fill it back up. I help them take accountability for both their wins and their losses. I ensure all know that my children have me in their corner—always. That I love them no matter what they do or who they become. That their power is theirs alone to keep or share. I am humbled in watching my own children share their gifts with other kids who need it. My daughter Lena befriended a child who was being picked on, then stood up in class putting all bullies on notice: if you bully her friend, you are bullying her, and that will not be tolerated. My other daughter, Bella, chooses not to listen to gossip as this is wrong and hurtful. Raff took the time to lend his power of understanding to kids who are challenged and need a friend. Why can't we all behave like children?

I love to see a young girl go out and grab the world by the lapels.
Life's a bitch.
You've got to go out and kick ass.

Maya Angelou

SHIFTING PARADIGMS

Do you have personal power? What does it look like to you? How do you show it off? Is it positive or negative? Who do you know that demonstrates strong personal power, and how do they do it? What are the results?

Power to make something impossible happen is a very sophisticated form of power. It is completely different from the forms of power that most people, even successful people, have learned during the course of their lives. It bears no relation to authority.... It has nothing to do with competence.... And it does not require influence.... When you acquire this power, you are free to take the risks and actions necessary to change the world.

Tracy Goss, author of *The Last Word on Power*

Grabbing Your Personal Power and Thriving. Personal Power is an ongoing learning process that pivots throughout life. I have listed ten tools that will help you gain and keep your power. This asset is so imperative for happiness that I recommend keeping a power book. I have a bright and colorful note book; its cover states "I am fairly certain that given a cape and a nice tiara, I could save the world." This is my Power Journal and in it I have the ten steps below, as well as examples and where I have struggled (when I gave my power away).

http://www.curlygirldesign.com/

Know your values. What are your values in life? I am betting you have never written them down. Your values are what internally drive you. They can be spiritual, ethical, personal, and inspirational. Think back to a time when you were the happiest; what was driving that internally? In listing your values, you make a statement. This is the core that drives me. Belief in God or divinity, to steal or not, to gossip or keep quiet, these are the rules by which you live and hold the bar for decisions. If you are finding yourself stepping out of the value circle, bring yourself back, forgive yourself and then make amends. Live by your values and you will sleep better at night.

One of the most courageous things you can do is identify yourself, know who you are, what you believe in & where you want to go.

Sheila Murray Bethel

Understand what you bring to the table. What are you good at? Are you a good negotiator, singer, dancer, writer? What are you passionate about—do you love blogging about food and wine? Is there something you want to do and have not done it? How do people relate to you—are you easy going or a bit of a strong-headed woman? How do you communicate? This is all about your strengths and where you wish to focus more time on—yourself. It is ALL about you.

The only person you can change is You...So let us focus there.

Be Fearless. Do not give into fear. It is an emotion that can run your life if you let it. Set your goals high and then go after them. I often tell my soccer and lacrosse teams, when facing a more aggressive team, "Do not be afraid of winning. Walk on the field as if you own it—at the end of the game, you will!"

Brand Yourself. You are reading that correctly. How people see you is your brand. How do you want people to see you? Compile a list of those traits and then confirm with some of your closest friends. Ah, be careful to understand why you want to be seen that way. Living within your values helps to shape you brand. Anyone who knows me would state "You always know where you stand with Lauran Star, she is direct and wastes no time selflessly giving of herself." Okay, there may be some truth to that statement—HA. I am direct and love empowering others.

Be You, everyone else is taken. Self-confidence is the intersection of personal power. You cannot be self-confident if you are wearing masks all the time. Be yourself; what is the worst that can happen, some people walk away? Guess what: they were never meant to be close to begin with. Embrace you! It is your individualism that guides your power; without that you are just a shadow of another.

Stop making excuses. There is no time like the present. You have to live in your power. If you read chapter one, hopefully you are moving beyond victim and survivor. If you are thriving you are no longer making up reasons for the barricades that hold you back.

Keep your power. The choice to keep it or give it away is all up to you. Whether it is in conflict resolution, asking for what you need, taking a stance on an issue or climbing the ladder of success, we make unconscious choices to either keep or hand our power over to the stronger party. We let them run the issues through pushing our hot buttons, threats, and negative self-talk, all just waiting to see our reactions. Stop reacting—take your ball and breathe. If you feel your power being infringed upon, take a break or walk away. It is perfectly fine to say to another, "I need a minute to compose my thoughts; can we pick this up in about __ minutes?" This works both at work and at home, with the PTA and with friendships. You just have to think before you react and hand your power over.

The glass is full. How full is your glass? Are you an optimist or pessimist? The shift is really quite easy. I wear many invisible glasses; my rose-colored ones are when life is down and I need to see the bright colors outside, and my prism glasses are for when life has handed me lemons and I need to shift my perspective to see the positive. However, it is more than shifting our vantage point, as we have to believe what we see. Embrace the other side of the argument before you make a decision. If your cake is half eaten, who can give you a slice or two?

Keep your eyes on others. With social media so available, who do you follow? I love Deepak Chopra, MD, Anthony Robbins, Gandhi and several other amazing people who focus on empowerment.

Help others find theirs. The best way to keep your power tuned in is by helping others find theirs. I noted earlier I coach youth girls sports. I do this for a variety of reasons, the largest being I not only coach these girls, I help them find their own power—that inner strength. They all know they have Coach R in their corner no matter what, and I believe in them. I get more from coaching them than they will ever know, as I have learned how to uncover my own strengths, to be silly and act like a child, to be resilient, and through all this, my goose bumps grow. How are you helping others find their power?

Personal power is as important as it is the foundation of taking charge of your life. The cornerstone to being your own CEO or Leading Your Own Ship. We are born with this skill set and then through life we learn to keep it or let it go. It goes beyond letting others define you—it is how YOU limit yourself, or not. Personal Power is the Fulcrum of success! It is the balance monitor. You decide whether to increase it or give it away. Do you willingly hand it over to the cake eaters or keep the slice for yourself?

Either Get on My Train or Get Off

As the quote says, either get on or get off; regardless, stop wasting time.

Hopefully this book has taken you on an amazing journey, one that will last a lifetime. You now have the tools to pivot your perspective both at home and in the workplace. You can step away from victim mode and move forward to thrive.

Define your needs both at home and at work, as well as understand the gender differences and embrace them. You can stop the battles at work and home around balance and have your cake and eat it too. When hard times fall upon you, you can get up and be resilient and get back in the saddle. Surely by now, in the end you have uncovered your strengths and areas for growth to say the least.

I have a saying in my house when I am facing something new and challenging, a new passage or chapter in my life that I am about to embark on. You can either get on my train—woo woo!—or get off. I do not say this lightly, as those who know and love me know I am jumping in with two feet. Whether it is a new book, new focus in life, or a new attitude, once I embrace this change, all around me have a choice that I cannot make for them. They are either supporting me or not—regardless, I am moving forward.

I have learned the hard way many people in our lives do not wish for our change. It is not because they are mean or do not wish us well—just the opposite, as it has nothing to do with us. They have to own it, not me. It is their own personal fear of change. If you take on their fear then you will not move forward. You have to recognize that concern for what it is and then make the choice to either survive or thrive. Once you yourself are empowered for change, you can then choose to empower those around you or let them find their own way.

Your empowerment takes work and is contagious, as it is also very scary not just for yourself but others who just are unsure they will gravitate to the new you. The frank aspect is, there is no new you. You are you, but today versus yesterday, you are stronger and more defined in what you desire from this life.

At the end of the day, we have the option to either be empowered or not, to survive or thrive. To that end, those around you also have a decision to make—should they jump on your train and enjoy the amazing journey with you, or should they get off? This is a difficult reflection of those in your life as some will let you down and other will step up.

I hope you thrive.

References

Adler, N. (2006). Coaching Executives: Women Succeeding Globally. *Coaching for leadership: The practice of leadership coaching from the world's greatest coaches (2nd ed.)* (pp. 237-244). San Diego, CA US: Pfeiffer & Company.

Alexander, B., 2014. Sorry Guys; Up to 80% of Women Fake It. MSNBC

Bar-On, Reuven and Parker, J. (2000). The Handbook of Emotional Intelligence: Theory, Development, Assessment and Application at Home, School and in the Workplace. Jossey-Bass.

Baxter, J., and E. O. Wright. "THE GLASS CEILING HYPOTHESIS: A Comparative Study of the United States, Sweden, and Australia." Gender & Society 14.2 (2000): 275-94. Social Science Computing Cooperative. University of Wisconsin - Madison

Bass, Bernard (2008). *Bass & Stogdill's Handbook of Leadership: Theory, Research & Managerial Applications* (4th ed.). New York, NY: The Free Press.

Belsten, L. (2006). Coaching Emotional Intelligence: The Art and Science of Accelerating the Achievements of Your Clients. CO; Boulder: Learnmore Communications Inc.

Brandt, Tiina, and Laiho. "Gender and Personality in Transformational Leadership Context." Leadership & Organization Development Journal 34.1 (2013): 44-66.

Brown, W., Bryant, S. & Reilly, M. (2006). Does emotional intelligence - as measured by the EQI - influence transformational leadership and/or desirable outcomes? *Leadership & Organization Development Journal, 27*(5), 330-351.

Brene Brown (2012). Daring Greatly: How the Courage to Be Vulnerable Transforms the Way We Live, Love, Parent, and Lead. Gotham Publishing

Cole, (2014). What our recent obsession of mindfulness really means. Fast Company May 14, 2014.

Duncan, P.(2007). Women in positions of leadership and gender-specific emotional intelligence attributes. Ph.D. dissertation, University of the Incarnate Word, United States -- Texas.

Edwards, G., (2014). *7 Leadership Styles and Famous Examples.*

Goleman, D. (2006). *Working with Emotional Intelligence.* NYNY: Bantam Dell

Goleman, D., Boyatzis, R., McKee, A. (2002) *Primal Leadership: Realizing the Power of Emotional Intelligence.* Boston, MA: Harvard Business School Press.

House. R.J., Dorfman, P., and Javidan, M. (2001). Project GLOBE: An Introduction. *Applied Psychology*, 50(4), 489-505.

Lichtenstein, B., & Plowman, D. (2009). The leadership of emergence: A complex systems leadership theory of emergence at successive organizational levels. *Leadership Quarterly*, *20*(4), 617-630.

Lopez-Zafra, Esther, Rocio Garcia-Retamero, and M. P. Martos. (2012). "THE RELATIONSHIP BETWEEN TRANSFORMATIONAL LEADERSHIP AND EMOTIONAL INTELLIGENCE FROM A GENDERED APPROACH." The Psychological Record 62.1 97-114.

Motherhood Today; Tougher Challenges less Success.

Manning, K. (2009). Increasing Women's Senior-Level Leadership in Student Affairs. *Student Affairs Leader*, *37*(23), 6-3

Mandell, B. & Pherwani, S. (2003). Relationship between Emotional Intelligence and Transformational Leadership Style: A Gender Comparison. *Journal of Business and Psychology, 17*(3), 387.

Murray, Sarah, and Milhausen. "Factors Impacting Women's Sexual Desire: Examining Long-Term Relationships in Emerging Adulthood." The Canadian Journal of Human Sexuality 21.2 (2012): 101-15.

Regins & Cotton. Easier Said Than Done: Gender differences in Perceived Barriers to Gaining a Mentor. Academi of Management Journal, (2014) ISSN: 0001-4273

Reuvers, M., van Engen, M., Vinkenburg, C., & Wilson-Evered, E. (2008). Transformational Leadership and Innovative Work Behavior: Exploring the Relevance of Gender Differences. *Creativity & Innovation Management*, *17*(3), 227-244.

Roche., Much Ado about Mentors. Harvard Business Review

Russo, Giovanni, and Hassink. "Multiple Glass Ceilings." Industrial Relations 51.4 (2012): 892-915. Business Source Premier..

Silverthorne, C. (2005). *Organizational Psychology in Cross Cultural Perspectives*. New York, New York: New York University Press.

Star, L., 2012. *LEIP Forward, Gaining Emotional Intelligence for Today Women Leader.* Sweet Dream Publishing

Warner, Judith. "Fact Sheet: The Women's Leadership Gap." Center for American Progress. N.p., 7 Mar. 2014.

Wattis, Louise, Kay Standing, and Mara A. Yerkes. "Mothers And Work–Life Balance: Exploring The Contradictions And Complexities Involved In Work–Family Negotiation." Community, Work & Family 16.1 (2013): 1-19. Family & Society Studies Worldwide.

Wiese, Bettina S., and Johannes O. Ritter. "Timing Matters: Length Of Leave And Working Mothers' Daily Reentry Regrets." Developmental Psychology 48.6 (2012): 1797-1807. Family & Society Studies Worldwide.

Uma D., J., & Glenice J., W. (2006). The role of leadership theory in raising the profile of women in management. *Equal Opportunities International, 25*(4), 236-250.

Pivotal Books I Love

I get asked, so what is on your book shelf? Well, here is what is on it right now...

301 Smart Answers to Tough Interview Questions by Vicky Oliver

Bad Bosses, Crazy Coworkers & Other Office Idiots: 201 Smart Ways to Handle the Toughest People Issues by Vicky Oliver

Emotional Resilience: Learn How to Be Resilient and Recover Quickly from Disappointment and Failure –Ebook. By Lisa Brighton.

For Women Only by Shaunti Feldhahn

For Men Only by Shaunti Feldhahn

Healthy Sex Drive, Healthy You: What Your Libido Reveals About Your Life by Diana Hoppe M.D.

Pushback: How Smart Women Ask—and Stand Up—for What They Want by Selena Rezvani

*Self-Awareness: How To Spot And Change Your Own Behavior and Disempowering Beliefs With A Proven Step-By-Step Formula For Dramatically Improving You Self ... Of Your Lif*e by Allan Twain

Stiletto Network: Inside the Women's Power Circles That Are Changing the Face of Business by Pamela Ryckman

The Female Brain by Louann Brizendine, M.D.

The Last Word on Power by Tracy Goss

The Next Generation of Women Leaders: What You Need to Lead but Won't Learn in Business School by Selena Rezvani

The Tapping Solution: A Revolutionary System for Stress-Free Living by Nick Ortner

About Lauran Star

Lauran Star is a sought after thought leader in Leadership Diversity and Women's Empowerment. Her leadership experience began in 1989 when Lauran became a proud member of the United States Armed Forces. With over fifteen years of leadership development with several Fortune 100 companies, Lauran understands what women need to thrive both in the business world and at home.

In the boardroom, she is the CEO of LS Consulting Group focused on Leadership Diversity, an international speaker and author. Her academic background includes a Master's Degree in Organizational Psychology, certified executive coach and licensed in several different assessments.

In the bedroom, Lauran Star is married and the proud mother of three children, residing in New Hampshire.
When Lauran Star is not speaking, writing, or consulting, you can find her on the girls' soccer or lacrosse field coaching.

To reach out to Lauran Star go to <u>www.LauranStar.com</u>

Lauran Star

93198450R00163

Made in the USA
Columbia, SC
07 April 2018